EXPLAINING THE INEXPLICABLE

ALSO BY THE RODENT

Rodent, Run

Rodent at Rest

Rodent Is Rich

Rodent Redux

Of Mice and Men

Beavers and Other Pond Dwellers

Gophers: Their Extraordinary Lives and Curious History

King Rat

Gerbils and Other Small Pets

Guinea Pig Children

Guinea Pigs No More!

Hamsters: An Owner's Guide to Choosing, Raising, Breeding and Showing

Squirrels in Britain

The Chipmunk Who Went to Church

Woodchucks and Their Kin

EXPLAINING THE INEXPLICABLE

by
The Rodent

POCKET BOOKS
New York London Toronto Sydney Tokyo Singapore

POCKET BOOKS, a division of Simon & Schuster Inc.
1230 Avenue of the Americas, New York, NY 10020

Original illustrations by Catherine Leary
Photographs by Margo Vann

Special thanks for the good humor of all the models whose photos appear in this book.

Library of Congress Cataloging-in-Publication Data

Rodent (Attorney)
Explaining the inexplicable: the Rodent's guide to lawyers / by the Rodent.
p. cm.
ISBN 0-671-52294-9
1. Lawyers—United States—Humor. 2. Practice of law—United States—Anecdotes. I. Title. II. Title: Rodent's guide to lawyers.
K184.R63 1995
340'.023'73—dc20 95-14587
CIP

Book design by Richard Oriolo

First Pocket Books hardcover printing August 1995

10 9 8 7 6 5 4 3 2 1

Printed in the U.S.A.

Contents

2

Infesting The Firm 33

3

Inside the Maze: Law Firm Life 53

FOREWORD

Let me explain . . .

Some things in life just can't be explained. What, for instance, caused the dinosaurs to become extinct? Why, during the winter of 1942 to 1943, did Hitler refuse to retreat from Stalingrad and thus subject his troops to a devastating and apparently unnecessary pounding at the hands of the Russians? Why do aliens always seem to land their space craft in remote rural areas? It seems far more logical that they would be attracted to the lights of big cities, doesn't it? These and other mysteries of the universe remain unexplained.

At the time I started law school, I began to notice many more apparently inexplicable phenomena. I am not referring simply to the esoteric and arcane concepts they teach in law school or the obscure legal issues I encountered while practicing law. I speak of far more curious things:

- Why did my classmates, who entered law school in hopes of ending social injustice wherever it exists, just three years later choose among jobs at corporate law firms based solely on which one offered the highest starting salary?

- Why do some states flunk two thirds of those taking the bar examination while trained monkeys could easily pass the exam in other states?

- Once I started to practice law, why was it that my true adversaries were not opposing counsel but rather my "colleagues" in my own firm who were trying to sabotage my career?

- Why did hardworking and competent lawyers struggle in the law firm environment while other, seemingly dim-witted and lazy lawyers thrive?

- Why did most of the lawyers I worked with prefer to spend all of their time at the office instead of with their families and friends?

As a young lawyer, I had no place to turn to find answers to these difficult questions. Such things are not taught in law school and, at the time, there were no books written on these matters. Even if the people I worked with actually knew the answers, they would only give me misinformation so as to throw me off my career track. All I could do was observe and try to figure things out for myself.

Working at a law firm consisting of eighteen hundred lawyers, I had ample opportunity to examine and evaluate lawyers and their behavior. Having accumulated valuable information from my exposure to so many attorneys, I decided to share my law firm knowledge with others. I tried to explain.

My original vessel of knowledge and commentary on law firm life was a newsletter entitled *The Rodent*. Knowing the firm's big cheeses would not take kindly to my missive, I published the newsletter anonymously and distributed copies around the office at four or five in the morning when most of my colleagues were at home.

Because the newsletter focused on issues that the firm's partners wished to remain unexplained, they tried to trap and exterminate *The Rodent*. As this game of cat and mouse grew more intense, I took drastic measures to protect my identity as the person behind the newsletter.

The firm began to review records of all large copying jobs done on their Xerox machines. Because each of us was required to use an individual code to access the office Xerox machines, the firm had records of all copies made and their dates. Anticipating this, I managed to obtain another lawyer's access code and use it when I reproduced the newsletter. When the firm's partners identified the unauthorized copying jobs corresponding to the dates *The Rodent* was distributed, they were sure they had their culprit. They had to rethink things, however, when their investigation led them directly to the firm's senior partner whose access code I had used.

Foiled again, the partners appointed someone to review individual computer files in hopes of finding the source. I was tipped off to this plan, however, and stored the newsletter's computer files on the directory of one of the firm's really pompous lawyers whom no one liked. This gave me a reprieve as it took quite a while for the unsuspecting lawyer to convince the partners he was not the vermin they were looking for.

Via plain envelopes, fax machines, and covert hand-offs, *The Rodent* newsletter eventually infested other law firms and is now read by thousands of lawyers from around the world. *The Rodent* not only is the voice of disenchanted lawyers but also is widely read by paralegals, legal secretaries, clients, law students, and lawyer families and friends (and enemies!) who need an explanation.

Those who used to describe their floundering legal careers by saying "I fought the law and the law won," now explain their success by saying: "I read it in *The Rodent.*"

Don't get trapped in the rat race when you can run with The Rodent!

Editor's Note: Only limited and SPCA-supervised testing of laboratory animals was conducted in conjunction with the compilation of this book.

Introduction: Explaining the Inexplicable

Lawyers are like the French, it's just our culture.

—American Bar Association's response to charges
that lawyers are obnoxious and annoying
(*The Rodent* newsletter, September 1993)

In addition to resembling the French, lawyers are also like the rich: they are different. "Different" might be an extremely generous way to describe lawyers and many people would choose other words—words that aren't even in the dictionary—to express their opinions of attorneys.

To be fair, lawyers themselves are not totally to blame for the way they are. All people are the product of their environment and lawyers have their own schools, language, television shows, fashion, annoying habits, goals, needs, and desires. These are the things that make up the Lawyer Culture and that need to be explained so that nonlawyers may better understand why lawyers are the way they are, that is, like the French. (You can imagine how frightening the combination of being French and a lawyer might be. French lawyers, however, while pretty terrible, are not as bad as New York lawyers.)

Individuals preparing to travel to a foreign country, such as France, or who are simply interested in different cultures often utilize guide books to learn about the language and customs of other peoples. Until now, there was no way to do the same when delving into the Lawyer Culture. *Ipso facto* (Latin and Lawyerese for "by this fact itself"), you hold before you *Explaining the Inexplicable: The Rodent's Guide to Lawyers.*

If you are not a lawyer, *The Rodent's Guide to Lawyers* will tell you everything you wanted to know about the legal profession but didn't want to be charged $250 an hour to find out. If you are a lawyer, this book and the outrageous and derogatory statements made about lawyers herein (Lawyerese for "here"), might be the subject of your next lawsuit. You should remember, however, that truth is an absolute defense to a legal claim of defamation.

Within any culture, there are subcultures and it is therefore inaccurate and unfair to make gross generalizations about all members of the Lawyer Culture. For this reason, *The Rodent's Guide to Lawyers* for the most part excludes the small percentage of attorneys whose purposes in practicing law are other than to become rich and contentious. District attorneys, public defenders, government lawyers, lawyers who work in-house for one company, lawyers who write newsletters and books making fun of lawyers, law professors, and a few others are mentioned only in passing. The Rodent's gross generalizations are saved for those to whom they can be accurately applied. These are the vast majority of lawyers who devote their lives to thriving at "The Firm."

The Firm is a hotbed of overcharged clients, overpaid lawyers, and oversized egos. It is often a large entity consisting of many attorneys representing huge corporate clients. The Firm may also be a smaller private practice representing small businesses and individuals. In fact, it can even be a sole proprietorship if it is operated by a lawyer with the right attitude.

It's extremely difficult to get into The Firm, and it's even harder to stay therein (Lawyerese for "there"), but most lawyers die therein. This is the story of that inexplicable place and its people.

BREEDING: A LAWYER IS BORN

Unlike most people who select their professions as young adults, lawyers are usually born to the bar. In fact, lawyerhood involves all aspects of life, which makes lawyers easily identifiable members of society. While it's virtually impossible, for example, to distinguish a grocer, bus driver, real estate appraiser, or even a paralegal among a group of people, attorneys have certain personality quirks and habits directly attributable to their livelihood.

Rodent's Firmiliar Quotations

I never met a lawyer.

—Will Rogers

One simple rule of thumb is that those who act like lawyers invariably *are* lawyers. You can confirm your suspicions upon meeting someone who acts like a lawyer by simply stating, "You must be a lawyer" (meaning, you're an asshole). Lawyers are always proud to be recognized and will quickly admit to their profession if correctly identified.

As the road to The Firm is a long one strewn with land mines, booby traps, and fallen competitors, future lawyers must begin the journey very early in life. Everything from school yard games to choice of playmates must be viewed with an eye toward a career in the law.

The steps along the way to The Firm are carved in stone. First, you must gain admission to a prestigious university, then earn high grades and score well on the Law School Admissions Test, and finally graduate at the top of your law school class in order to qualify for a job with The Firm. Then you must survive for years as an associate in order to be elected partner.

Because there's so much to do, and because lawyers charge by the hour, there's no time to waste in getting started. Farewell youth! Hello prelawyerhood!

Rodent Tale

During a session of a panel organized by the American Bar Association, a lawyer from the law firm Skadden, Arps, Slate, Meagher & Flom advocated a litigation technique that other panel members found questionable. When the panel's moderator pressed the lawyer about her comments, she responded, "Don't forget, I'm at Skadden, Arps now. We pride ourselves on being assholes. It's part of the firm culture."

The Young and the Contentious

Attorneys are often asked the question: "When did you know you wanted to be a lawyer?" Sometimes the answer is: "After I couldn't get into medical school, even one of the foreign ones." More often than not, however, the response is "I've *always* wanted to be a lawyer."

Baby Barristers are recognizable from the moment of birth. Telltale signs the youngster will grow up to practice law for a living and that child abandonment might be the most attractive option for parents, include:

- Demanding cash up front in lieu of mother's milk.
- Irritation and excessive crying when there's nothing really wrong.
- Learning to whine before learning how to talk.

As Baby Barristers grow older, lawyerly tendencies become more prevalent. Kid Attorneys develop their own particular tastes and ways of doing things. Here are some warning signs:

- Of all the things at the aquarium, they like sharks the best.
- They run for and are elected class president (only to be impeached later).
- They become best friends with the kids in the class who want to be ambulance drivers when they grow up.
- They tend to double-bill parents for their weekly allowance.

▪ *Childhood Lawyer Games* ▪

Normal Healthy Child	*Lawyer of the Future*
Cowboys and Indians	Plaintiffs and Defendants
Spin the Bottle	Sexual Harassment
Doctor	Medical Malpractice Attorney
Truth or Dare	Admission or Perjury
Kick the Can	Kick Opposing Counsel's Ass
Show and Tell	Bill and Collect
Hopscotch	Scotch on the Rocks
House	Asbestos-Infested House with Faulty Design and Foundation
G.I. Joe	*Homosexual G.I. Plaintiff* v. *U.S. Army*

▪ *Attorney Egometer* ▪

It remains a great legal mystery as to which came first, the big ego or the lawyer. Most people nevertheless agree that another distinguishing attorney characteristic is an immense yet fragile ego.

During the course of a legal career, all lawyers experience events dramatically affecting their financial status, reputation, and personal lives. Always hardest hit, however, are their egos. The Attorney Egometer can help to monitor these career disruptions and enhance readers' understanding of their effects.

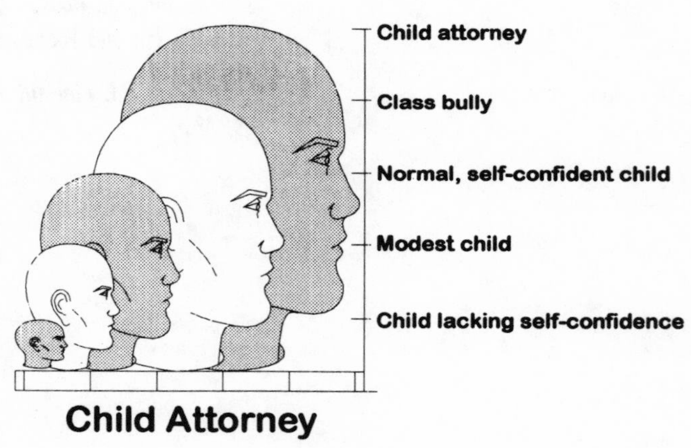

Child Attorney

Rodent Tale

To thrive in the legal world, attorneys must not only make The Firm their life but also score high on the Egometer. As an associate from one of the biggest law firms put it, ". . . this isn't what I do from eight to five. It's who or what I am." This lawyer went on to say that his white shirt and rep tie are "like a second skin" and the Milbank, Tweed lawyer is the quintessence of rectitude—"We're just better than you. It's not just that we're better lawyers, it's just that we're better as a person in a moral sense."

This Way to Law School

The early years of a lawyer's life are devoted to getting into a top law school. This is critical because The Firm hires only graduates of the few best schools. Waiting too long to prepare or missing a step along the way to law school means ending up at a mediocre institution. Graduating from a mediocre law school means forfeiting the opportunity to be considered for a job with The Firm and, most likely, ending up wasting your life charging less than $350 an hour for legal services.

Although law school is years away, the Prelawyer's carefree days of childhood quickly give way to plans for admission to just the right institution. Most of those who are eventually hired by The Firm take the following steps on the way to law school.

Rodent Tale

When the United States was selected to host the World Cup in 1994, Attorney Alan Rothenberg was appointed head of World Cup USA '94 and given primary responsibility for the event.

With such a big job ahead of him, Attorney Rothenberg knew he had to inspire his staff. He therefore set a goal for them. The goal Attorney Rothenberg set for the World Cup staff was to get *him* in the top ten of *The Sporting News* list of the hundred most powerful sports people. "Start working on it now," he ordered.

At the time the goal was set, Attorney Rothenberg was number 95 on the *Sporting News* list. Instead of getting to the top of the list, Attorney Rothenberg was taken off the list entirely. The editor of *The Sporting News* explained that "it just doesn't appear to us that Rothenberg has that much power."

Rodent Tale

The American Lawyer magazine published an extensive article on John Johnson, a partner in the Dallas law firm of Johnson & Gibbs. The article is entitled "Johnny Juggernaut" and Attorney Johnson is described as "No Mr. Nice Guy. But the aggressive real estate specialist has not let his personality stop him from masterminding the firm's spectacular growth."

While he may not be Mr. Nice Guy (he is reportedly in the habit of throwing sharpened pencils at his secretary), Attorney Johnson certainly scores nicely on the Egometer. He is quoted in the article as saying: "I don't trust anybody's judgment but my own and I don't recall ever making a mistake." (Johnson denies making the statement. If he did, he says, he said it in jest.) Another Johnson & Gibbs partner recounts trying to explain a new phone system to Attorney Johnson. The lawyer explained that to reach Arthur Hewett, the firm's managing partner, a caller should push the number 1. "Johnson immediately demanded to know what number he needed to reach his own line," the partner remembered. When Attorney Johnson was told his number was 2, he belted out: "Why am I number two and Hewett number one?"

Step 1.
▪ *Admission to the Right College* ▪

College is nothing more than a stepping stone to law school. The Teenage Attorney can take either of two paths leading to admission to one of the few law schools deemed acceptable by The Firm.

Plan A. One way to get into a choice university is by working hard, perhaps winning a scholarship to a prep school and earning good grades. Although some people claim to admire hard work, Plan A (and hard work) is for suckers.

Plan B. The better and more effective path to getting into a good university is by using family connections. The folks' financing of a new wing to the university medical center and naming it after the applicant, for instance, will have a very positive impact on the admissions committee.

Rodent Tale

Attorney Nancy Ezold claimed that she was denied promotion at the Philadelphia firm of Wolf, Block because she is a woman. When she sued the firm, Wolf, Block responded by saying one of the main reasons Attorney Ezold was not elected partner was because she attended law school at Villanova. Villanova, the firm pointed out, is considered a second-tier law school.

One of the firm's former partners said that Ezold "could never overcome the prejudice of her law school record, which is like walking around with a yellow star on your arm. You can't overcome that."

Another partner described Attorney Ezold's situation this way: "It's like the ugly girl. Everybody says she's got a great personality. It turns out, [Ezold] didn't even have a great personality."

Step 2.
▪ *The Law School Application* ▪

The law school application provides an excellent chance for Prelawyers to show law schools how good they really are. The best opportunity to display your talents is in the section of the application requesting a list of academic and community achievements. Law schools rarely bother verifying these matters and the Prelawyer's only limitations are those of imagination. Most Prelawyers take the time to describe the extensive scope of their involvement with a number of bogus community groups in an effort to appear "well-rounded."

Another part of the application just begging for embellishment is the section requesting personal references. Successful applicants usually list individuals who are well-known yet unreachable for confirmation. Reclusive celebrities and recently deceased members of the U.S. Supreme Court are excellent references and can also be used later in legal life on a résumé. It's also helpful to mention that the applicant is a direct descendent of the person who founded that particular university.

Rodent Tale

Attorney Edward Yodowitz was hired as a managing clerk, not as a lawyer, at a major law firm. Although his job responsibilities were primarily clerical, Mr. Yodowitz sometimes volunteered to help out associates with their work and was occasionally asked to put in overtime doing research for legal articles.

When Mr. Yodowitz, a graduate of the University of Baltimore School of Law, where he was an average student, expressed that he would like to try his hand as an associate, some of the firm's lawyers greeted the request skeptically. "This isn't 'Cinderella,'" he was told by one lawyer. He was later granted his request.

APPLICATION FOR ADMISSION

14. Awards and Scholarships. Please list below all academic, civic and community scholarships and citations for which you have been recognized.

Nobel Peace Prize, Presidential Medal of Freedom, three-time singles winner at Wimbledon, Purple Heart, Rodent's Person of the Fiscal Year (FY 1992–93), Pulitzer Prize, Olympic Gold Medal and personal friend of Barbra Streisand.

22. Personal References. In the space provided below, please list individuals who know you well and who we can contact as personal references.

1. Salman Rushdie
2. Roman Polanski
3. Jimmy Hoffa
4. Michael Rockefeller
5. Queen Elizabeth II

Step 3.
▪ *Suing the Law School* ▪

How dare they reject the Prelawyer! If the application is turned down, either (a) a terrible mistake has been made, (b) a few phone calls to the right people will remedy the situation, or (c) the law school can be sued and forced to admit the applicant.

Rodent Tale

The résumé of Los Angeles criminal defense attorney Dennis Palmieri indicated he was responsible for "dismantling the Berlin Wall, razing the Iron Curtain, unifying Germany, bringing democracy to Eastern Europe and individual republics of the Soviet Union." The same résumé failed to include a description of Attorney Palmieri's legal experience but did claim credit for the advocacy of a lunar mining colony, a Martian expedition, and "edifying re-examination of the Christian Principal in its substance and essence."

The content of the résumé was questioned when Attorney Palmieri served as counsel to a defendant in the case involving the beating of truck driver Reginald Denny in the aftermath of the first Rodney King verdict. In response, the lawyer reportedly said that others were out to destroy "Dennis the Great." "I am Dennis Palmieri the Great," he reportedly said, "and everyone knows me around the world." Palmieri denied calling himself "Dennis the Great," but another lawyer reported that Attorney Palmieri told her that "he was Jesus and that his enemies would be crucified."

Dennis the Great is a member in good standing of the California State Bar.

The Prelawyer should make it known up front that a rejection will be contested by retaining legal counsel to submit the application. The law school will feel it has no choice but to admit. Plus, having a prominent law firm on her side will ensure that they won't screw around with the Prelawyer's grades once she is admitted.

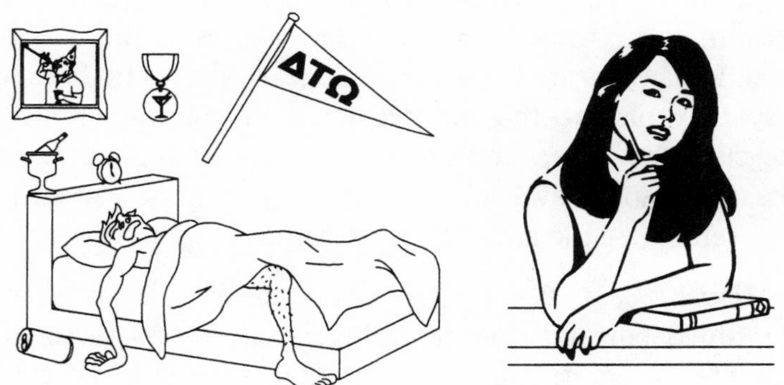

Prelawyers at Class Time

▪ *Greek Virtues* ▪

Once in college, the next important step in the Prelawyer's life is getting the grades necessary for acceptance to law school. The most successful future lawyers take the path of least resistance to the honor roll—they join a fraternity or sorority. These institutions are packed with Prelawyers primarily because the Greeks offer many benefits essential to those intent on attending law school.

The House Exam and Term Paper File. The Prelawyer knows that the college years are the prime of a young person's life and time is better spent partying with future clients than studying. At term paper time, instead of wasting countless hours in the library that could be better spent drunk, Greek future lawyers simply pick a term paper from the house's file and hand it in. (Don't forget to change the name on the cover page!) At finals time, there's another file full of last year's exams or a freshly stolen copy of the current term's exam.

Brothers and Sisters Know the Best Classes. Law schools discourage students from taking law classes at the college level. Prelawyers are therefore free to take classes that are so easy they obviate the inconvenience of coming up with recycled term papers and stolen examinations. A list of these classes is usually available from one of the house's seventh-year seniors or the athletic department.

House Social Events. The Greek system also provides plentiful opportunity to meet and eventually marry the son or daughter of a partner at The Firm. This is the most effective shortcut to The Firm and renders academic qualifications meaningless.

Learning to Drink and Being One of the Boys (Even If You're a Girl). Greek Prelawyers won't pick up much in the classroom but they will learn many far more useful skills. Holding one's liquor, for example, will impress both colleagues and clients and prove essential upon joining The Firm. Valuable experience is also gained in telling off-color jokes, recounting sexual escapades, and name dropping. All of these activities provide excellent training for the real world of lawyers.

▪ *"My First Law Fib"* ▪

Practicing law often presents situations in which the truth can cost you a certain amount of discomfort, embarrassment, and/or money. Members of the legal profession have therefore invented "Law Fibs" to protect themselves from such situations.

The Prelawyer's introduction to law fibbing often occurs upon the receipt of unhappy news from the law school admissions committee. If the Prelawyer can't get that wing of the university hospital built, doesn't get into a good fraternity or sorority, or if the data on the admissions application is checked and admission to the law school of choice is rejected, the next step is to protect one's reputation. Just one clever Law Fib can be extremely handy in convincing family, friends, and The Firm's recruiting committee that the Prelawyer is still Firm timber even after being rejected by all the best law schools.

- "I decided to turn down Stanford. Instead, I'm going to South Northeast West Virginia Valley State, which is actually ranked higher than Stanford and a much better law school."
- "Sure, Yale's fine if you like cold weather and want to be president or sit on the U.S. Supreme Court, but climate is what's important to me. That's why I chose The Jamaican School of Law."
- "I'm going to Harvard." (This Law Fib should be accompanied by a Law Prayer that no one comes to visit.)

Rodent Tale

In early 1994, the Chicago law firm Mayer, Brown put partner Richard Salomon on leave after the firm learned of an error on his résumé. This development took the legal world by surprise because Attorney Salomon was a law firm's dream, described as a "hard-driving, aggressive lawyer, who routinely billed more than 3,000 hours a year, often arriving at work between 3:00 A.M. and 4:00 A.M."

The fact that the firm took such an action is also surprising because, in the world of Law Fibs and résumé embellishment, this error was clearly in the minor leagues. Attorney Salomon's résumé stated that he graduated from Harvard Law School with honors when he in fact graduated from Harvard without honors.

The reasons behind the law firm's action became much clearer when it was learned that Attorney Salomon had been overbilling clients for disbursements. Mr. Salomon's attorney said a psychological impairment—compulsive neurosis, "compounded by the pressures that exist" in big law firms—was the cause of his client's conduct. Perhaps the real reason for Attorney Salomon's departure was explained by a former Mayer, Brown partner. "People hated him," the partner said. "He was obnoxious, abrupt, and didn't treat people well."

Student Lawyer

Once in law school, the scramble to succeed continues unabated as students vie for the good grades necessary to get a job interview with The Firm. Added to this pressure is the overwhelming law school workload and, most damning, the continual exposure to other lawyers-in-training. Within a few weeks of starting law school, the Student Lawyer is eating, drinking, sleeping, and breathing the law. Worst of all, the Student Lawyer starts to think like a lawyer.

Once again, the Student Lawyer is easily distinguished from other members of society.

Rodent Tale

"Your [spouses] are going to change: their personalities are going to change in law school. They'll get more aggressive, more hostile, more precise, more impatient."

—University of Chicago Law School administrator speaking to spouses of first-year law students.

▪ *Thinking like a Lawyer* ▪

Law School Study Group

To help manage the heavy workload of law school, industrious students form study groups. The idea behind a study group is for the members to pool their efforts and share their work.

While created with the best of intentions, students in competition with each other just aren't very good at cooperating. Almost every study group ends in disaster. Episodes of study group sabotage and double cross are common. It is here that law students learn the personal relations skills they take with them to The Firm. Members of the study group include:

The No Good/Do Good

Class Standing: Middle.

Contribution to Study Group: Reads all background material and researches everything in extensive detail.

Hobbies: Reading all background material and researching everything in extensive detail.

Reason for Attending Law School: To make the world a better place through use of the legal system.

Future in the Law: "Paper or plastic?" (Lost job with Habitat for Halibut due to lack of funding.)

Top of the Class

Class Standing: Number one.

Contribution to Study Group: Lectures others on finer points of the law she thinks they can't understand. When it comes time to share her work, she drops out of the study group because she wants to associate only with students in the top five percent of law school class. She drops her boyfriend for the same reason.

Hobbies: Hanging around after class to chat with professors.

Reason for Attending Law School: To get back at people who have been mean to her.

Future in the Law: Practices "environmental law" (Law Fibese for "counsel to toxic polluters").

Drunk and Stupid

Class Standing: Bottom.

Contribution to Study Group: Cocktails.

Hobbies: Violating the law school's honor code.

Reason for Attending Law School: College was over.

Future in the Law: Barely graduates from law school. Passes bar exam only after moving to Pennsylvania, where the test is really easy. Once practicing law, he thrives as a lawyer due to his unique ability to wine and dine clients and bring business to The Firm. His buddies elect him president of the state bar association.

▪ *Law Student Metamorphosis* ▪

Many Student Lawyers decide to attend law school because they want to make the world a better place. Upon learning how much The Firm pays its attorneys, however, Student Lawyers quickly realize their own personal worlds will be better if they go into private practice. Suddenly, using the legal system to end world hunger seems like just a big waste of time.

First Day of Law School

"I want to end poverty and social injustice wherever they exist."

End of First Year

"Greenpeace sounds good but I think it might be better to work at Legal Aid in case, God forbid, I go into private practice someday."

Second Year

"Corporate securities would be interesting and it might be good experience to start at a big firm."

Upon Graduation

"How do those bastards expect me to live on seventy-five thousand dollars a year?"

Rodent Tale

"What's wrong with yuppiedom? Even though I'm blond and wear pearls, I notice people gravitate toward me because I'm a law student. There is a certain built-in respect."

—Third-year law student, Duke University

"The promise of big bucks is important here. The only overriding element is a sense of competition. Ethics and principles rarely figure in . . ."

—Third-year law student, Vanderbilt University

"Why law? I want to be at the core of potential societal change. Law provides that, plus status and money."

—Second-year law student, Duke University

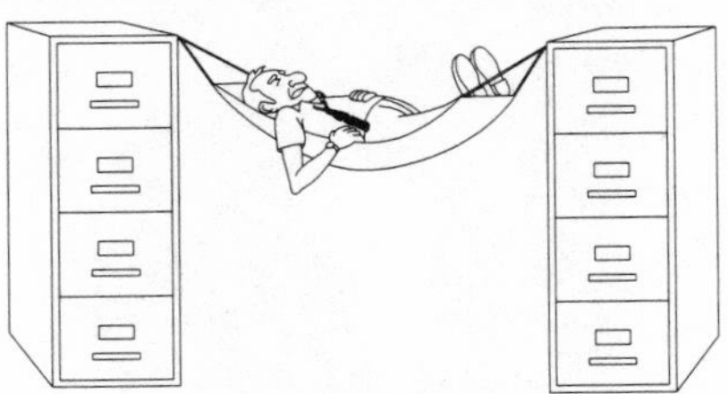

Summer Vacation

During the first and second years of law school, many law students interview with The Firm for positions as summer associates. Summer associates spend their vacation months at The Firm in order to decide if they would like to work there full-time upon graduation.

The Firm regards its summer associates very highly and some larger firms spend as much as a million dollars a year on the summer associate program. Primarily through food and drink, every effort is made to assure the honored guests that The Firm is a pleasant place to work. Lawyers are charged with the task of making The Firm look like a civilized environment.

As The Firm embarks on its annual summer charade, lawyers have to be reminded of how to behave while the vacationers are visiting.

Rodent Tale

The Committee on Civility of the United States Court of Appeals for the Seventh Circuit in Chicago issued a report devoting sixty pages to describing the degraded state to which lawyerly manners have slipped in recent years. The committee found lawyers to be rude, belligerent, manipulative, and deceitful to one another.

Looking for the reasons why the profession has declined as far as it has, the report quoted one lawyer who said that "sometime during the last fifteen years, many young persons entering law adopted the belief that lawyers were supposed to be rich and, lately, extravagantly rich. The greediest of the young lawyers," the attorney wrote, "were attracted to large firms that paid the highest salaries. Their relentless pursuit of money has virtually destroyed their ability to develop friendships with opposing lawyers."

THE FIRM

Internal Memorandum

TO: All Associates
FROM: The Recruiting Committee
RE: Summer Associates' Imminent Arrival

It's that time again! This year's crop of summer associates will be arriving shortly and, as always, each of us has to do his best to convince the youngsters they should join us upon graduation from law school. Please follow the guidelines below to ensure this year's summer program is a success.

1. Upon encountering a summer associate, even for the second or third time in the same day, always volunteer: "The Firm isn't a sweatshop. We care only about your professional development and emphasize a healthy working environment."

2. Any interesting, easy, and fun projects that include travel to exotic locations should be assigned to summer associates. Those projects involving the usual legal drudgery should continue to be assigned to junior associates.

3. Refrain from asking summer associates out on dates (this privilege is reserved for partners).

4. Tell summer associates believable stories to explain why none of the lawyers they interviewed with just a few months ago are still at The Firm.

5. In the presence of summer associates, refrain from using the profane and derogatory language commonly used at The Firm to describe other lawyers.

6. Always remember to distinguish between summer associates and first-year associates. Summer associates' work product—no matter how poor it is and even if you have to do the whole project over yourself—should always be received with elaborate praise. First-year associates should continue to be fired for producing anything less than perfect work.

7. If a summer associate threatens to report you or The Firm to the state bar for any of the many ethical violations he or she has observed, threaten back that you will have all information on the summer associate's résumé verified.

Rodent Tale

When told that some of his colleagues were thinking of leaving his firm, a senior partner from one of the biggest American law firms responded: "That's ridiculous. Let me tell you something. There are three reasons why they aren't leaving. One: they're too well paid. Two: they could never get another position of this caliber. Three: they are making too much money."

Rodent Tales

Every year, *The American Lawyer* magazine asks summer associates to complete a survey regarding their experiences at major law firms. Below are some of the more memorable responses about summer associate programs.

"I didn't do any work and I didn't get fired."

—Sonnenschein Carlin Nath & Rosenthal, Chicago

"We ate so much that someone suggested we ought to rename the firm 'Free Food.'"

—Fried, Frank, Harris, Shriver & Kampelman, Washington, D.C.

"I think I saw a client once—in the bathroom."

—Hale and Dorr, Boston.

"The closest I came to client contact this summer was being allowed to hear a client's voice over a speakerphone after being emphatically told to keep my mouth shut."

—Wilmer, Cutler & Pickering, Washington, D.C.

"Activities included an end-of-the-summer prom, a burrito-eating contest, horseback riding in the moonlight—and partners and associates alike doing combat in a wading pool full of cherry Jell-O."

—Loeb and Loeb, Los Angeles

"Given the money this place spends on the summer associate program, it seems to me that the firm would save itself a lot of trouble and heartache if, instead, it gave each of us a new Porsche."

—Isham, Lincoln & Beale, Chicago

Summer Associate Evaluations

It is pretty much a foregone conclusion that all summer associates, no matter how incompetent, will get offers for full-time employment upon graduation from law school. The real purpose of the summer program, therefore, is for The Firm to demonstrate just how fun practicing law can be. Summer associates are, however, evaluated based on the following:

1. Informal swimsuit competition at The Firm's summer pool party.

2. Utilization of The Firm's credit card for charging whatever the summer associate feels is appropriate for a night's entertainment. This helps evaluate skill in running up a tab when the client is paying. Evaluations are based on imagination and courage. In the past, points have been scored by charging such things as a semester's tuition and taking a Concorde to London for dinner.

3. Ability to hold one's liquor, recount sexual escapades, and tell off-color jokes and amusing personal stories. (You see, some of those things learned in college do prove useful later in life.)

2

Infesting The Firm

Immediately upon acceptance to law school, the law student's attention turns to legal life's next major challenge—landing a job.

A law degree offers many diverse career options such as teaching, working as in-house counsel for a company, representing a public interest or nonprofit organization, working for the government, forming a small firm with other lawyers, or opening up your own law office. If all else was equal, law

Rodent's Firmiliar Quotations

Life is short. Work hard.

—Advice from The Firm's senior partner to first-year associates

students would set their sights on any of these various types of legal service.

All else is not equal because The Firm pays the highest salaries to new lawyers. Thus, instead of considering what type of legal career would be most suitable for them, most law students maneuver for a job with The Firm.

Getting hired by The Firm demands complete focus. Just one misstep here and law students will end up representing small-time clients in litigation, ironically, against The Firm's lawyers. If a law student plays everything just right, she will get a job in a luxurious office in a downtown high-rise making more money than the student's parents ever dreamed of (unless, of course, her parents are partners at The Firm).

The Bar Examination

The culmination of a lawyer's academic career is the bar examination. Passing the exam is crucial because all lawyers, even the really bad ones, must pass in order to (legally) practice law.

The degree of difficulty associated with the bar exam depends upon where you take it. In California and New York, for instance, the test is extremely challenging and only about forty percent of the law school graduates pass it each time it is offered. In Pennsylvania, by contrast, the only way to fail the bar exam is by using the wrong type of lead pencil.

The bar examination is supposed to evaluate knowledge of the law, but its real purpose is to test the ability to sit in a room for long periods of time with unwashed future lawyers. The questions themselves are designed more to confuse and annoy the exam taker than to address knowledge of the law.

Rodent Tale

When her husband failed the bar examination, one California lawyer decided to come to his aid. She dressed up like a man and took the exam under her husband's name the next time it was offered.

Unfortunately for the couple, the wife's score was so much higher than her husband's failing score that it tipped off bar examiners. They investigated and discovered the fraud. The wife was disbarred and the couple divorced soon thereafter.

Rodent Tale

In most states, to pass the bar examination one must get a passing score on the standardized, national Multistate Bar Examination (MBE) as well as on essay questions and a practical performance segment of the exam. In a number of states, the exam is given over three days and consists of six hours of essay questions, six hours for performance tests, and six hours for the MBE.

In Pennsylvania, the exam is only two days long, and the second day often is meaningless. A candidate is guaranteed to pass the bar exam if she receives a minimum passing score on the MBE. Bar examiners in Pennsylvania do not even read the answers to the other parts of the exam if the candidate gets the minimum MBE score.

The difference between the states in this regard has led to a great migration across state lines at bar exam time, especially by those who plan to practice law in Washington, D.C. In fact, the vast majority of lawyers practicing law in Washington never take the District of Columbia bar exam. This is because the D.C. bar has one of the more challenging exams. At the same time, it is very easy to "waive into" the D.C. bar by becoming a member of any state bar and then filling out an application to be admitted in the District of Columbia.

"Our students wouldn't dream of sitting for the D.C. bar," said the dean of the District of Columbia School of Law. Instead, most flock to Pennsylvania at bar exam time. One lawyer who stayed in Washington to take the bar exam in order to show clients his commitment to the District told *The Washington Post,* "Of course, if I fail, my butt will be in Pennsylvania tomorrow."

▪ *Preparing for the Bar Examination* ▪

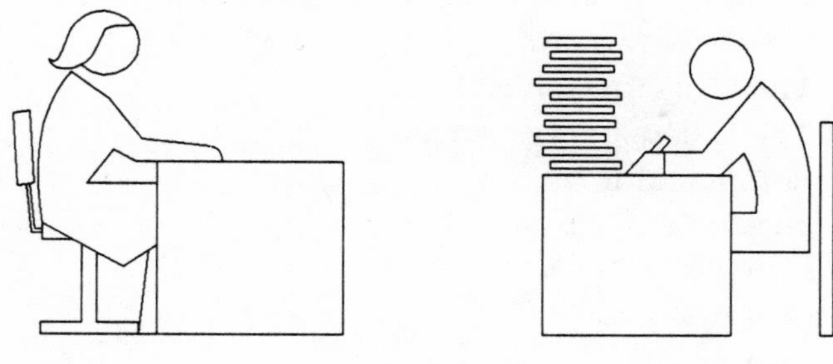

New York

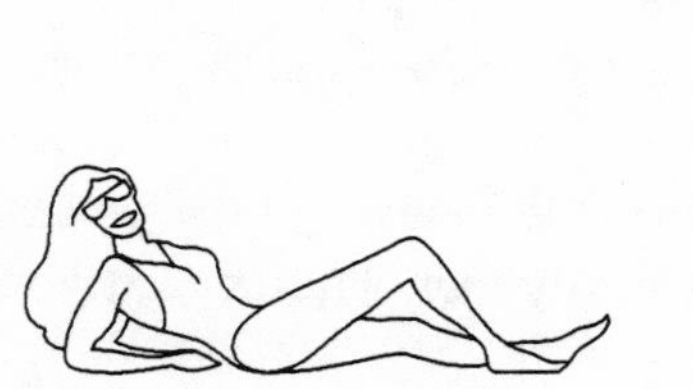

Pennsylvania

SAMPLE BAR EXAM QUESTIONS

1. The freedom to practice one's religion of choice is guaranteed by which amendment to the United States Constitution?
   a. The First Amendment.
   b. The Fourteenth Amendment.
   c. Both a and b.
   d. Neither a nor b.
   e. a but not b.
   f. b but not a.
   g. c but not d.
   h. e from Question 22 but not c from Question 39.
   i. i.

2. You are in the middle of an important meeting and your secretary interrupts to tell you that your spouse has just been in a serious accident and taken to the hospital. As a lawyer, you:
   a. Chastise your secretary for interrupting the meeting.
   b. Tell the other people in the meeting how you're not very happily married anyway. Thank God your secretary is okay.
   c. Brag that you'll soon be handling a big personal injury case.
   d. Send a paralegal or your five-year-old daughter to the hospital to cover for you.
   e. Start to laugh as if you believe your secretary is only joking, continue meeting.

3. (For those taking this examination in Pennsylvania only.) If you think you might have come within two letters of a correct answer on one of the previous questions, that's good enough for us! You passed and can go home now. Don't forget to pick up your license to practice law on the way out.

Rodent Tale

During the February 1992 California bar examination, one exam taker suffered a seizure. Five other applicants sitting nearby came to the man's aid until paramedics arrived.

The California Bar said it would give no special consideration or adjust the exam scores of those who helped the stricken man. Only after intense criticism in the press for the way it treated the Good Samaritans did the California Bar agree to take the incident into consideration when grading the exams. Eventually, the Bar gave each of them a special commendation.

▪ *Failing the Bar Exam* ▪

There are a number of troublesome problems associated with the bar examination. The biggest drawback is that it's very hard (but not impossible!) to cheat. This makes the exam especially burdensome for those who haven't studied a lick and got through law school on copies of stolen tests.

Another less-than-positive aspect of the exam is that, in many states, it takes months for the results to be announced. By this time, the Prelawyer has already started working at The Firm. This means that everyone at the office anticipates the results and looks forward to offering congratulations to the new lawyer.

For those who pass the bar exam, it's great fun coming to the office after the results have been announced and accepting the good wishes of colleagues. For those who fail the exam, it's not quite as much fun.

The worst part about failing the bar exam is breaking the news to The Firm's partners who hired the lawyer-who-may-never-be. Despite their obvious disappointment upon learning that someone they hired to practice law has not qualified to do so, partners make every effort to show sympathy for, and give encouragement to, the young associate who can now be found lying at the bottom of the Egometer.

Rodent Tale

When John F. Kennedy, Jr., failed the New York bar examination, the *New York Post* reported the event with the headline: THE HUNK FLUNKS! Dr. Joyce Brothers gave her thoughts on the issue: "I think he wants it (to pass the bar) desperately." The former president's son explained his predicament by saying: "I'm clearly not a legal genius."

On his third try, Mr. Kennedy passed the exam after he was reportedly allowed to take the test in a private room. Private rooms are usually reserved for those bar exam takers who are sick. This created some resentment on the part of other candidates. Said one: "Kennedy didn't look sick to me that day. In fact, he was playing Frisbee in the park afterwards with some girls."

Rodent Tales

Bar Flunkers Fun Facts:

- California's last three governors have taken a total of eight California bar examinations.
- After taking and failing the bar examination several times, Shakey Johnson gave up on becoming a lawyer and instead opened a pizza parlor named for himself. "Shakey's" ultimately became America's largest chain of pizza parlors.
- Although never reaching the prominence of Shakey Johnson, another noteworthy bar flunker was Charles Evans Hughes. After failing the New York bar examination six times, Charles Evans Hughes went on to become the Chief Justice of the United States Supreme Court.

What Partners Say to Associates Who Fail the Bar Exam

"Have you ever thought about making pizzas for a living?"

"We may have an opening in our Philadelphia office."

"Boy, what a blow to the old Egometer!"

"It could happen to anyone. Don't worry about it. You're fired."

"That's okay, I didn't pass either. In fact, I never took the exam. The Firm doesn't bother to verify attorney licenses."

"I thought you were a secretary. What the hell were you doing taking the bar exam anyway?"

ATTORNEY EGOMETER

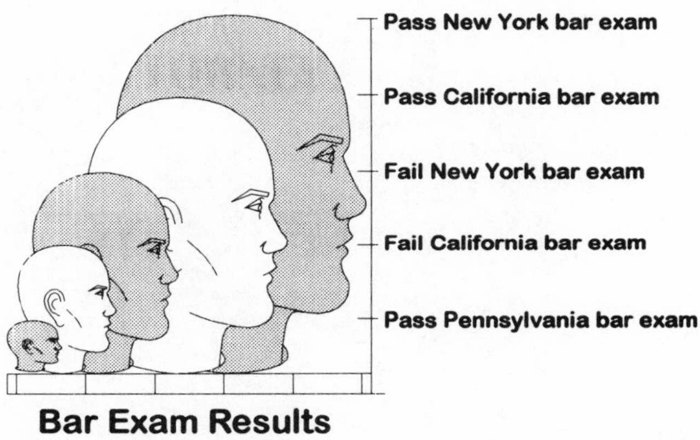

Rodent Tale

Six first-year associates at Philadelphia's Blank, Rome law firm were fired after failing the New Jersey bar examination. Each had previously taken and (obviously) passed the Pennsylvania bar exam. Only one of the six associates worked in the firm's New Jersey office.

A partner broke the news by telling the associates that he was an "elitist" and they were "embarrassments to the firm," according to one of the associates. The partner said those weren't the words he used, but added, "When we pay for people to take the test, we expect them to pass. I don't think that's an unreasonable expectation."

Options upon Failing ▪ *the Bar Exam* ▪

1. Law Fib. Say you passed and hope no one bothers to check. (If you get caught law fibbing, at least you won't be disbarred.)

2. Move to Pennsylvania. This should solve the problem. There is a risk, however, that comes with taking the exam in a state where almost everyone passes. While anyone can fail in one of the more difficult states, you'll expose yourself as a true idiot if you fail in one of the really easy states.

3. Join the Secret Society of Bar Failers. After you fail the bar exam, people whom you never met before will show up at your office, close the door, and admit that they too failed the exam. You will then be asked to join Bar

Flunkers Anonymous and attend the next meeting of the Charles Evans Hughes Secret Society of Bar Failers, where you'll learn the secret bar failers' nod and handshake.

Passage to The Firm

After years of preparation, but before actually beginning to practice law, future lawyers reach a critical stage in their lives. It is now time to be hired by The Firm.

If the soon-to-be lawyer has taken all the right steps along the way, she will be eligible for a job interview with The Firm. There will, however, be many other qualified law students vying for a limited number of positions with The Firm. The one thing separating those eventually hired by The Firm and those passed over is the ability to law fib. The successful applicant can demonstrate she is Firm timber by peppering her résumé and job interviews with winning Law Fibs.

While some may have reservations about not telling the truth (remember, these people are still only law students—not yet lawyers), it must be kept in mind that The Firm itself tells many Law Fibs during the recruiting process. While a recruit might embellish upon her law school grades, class standing, work experience, and commitment to the law ("I've always wanted to spend my life researching Montana's municipal bond law"), The Firm's lawyers will pretend to be nice people and claim The Firm is a pleasant place to work.

While the distinction between "lawyer" and "liar" is often blurred, the entire recruitment process revolves around the Law Fib. Best of all, since both sides know the other is lying, it is here that individuals can let loose with some of their best material. Fib freely!

▪ *The Interview* ▪

For those who take all the right steps along the way, interviewing is just a formality. Less fortunate candidates will have to endure real interviews with as many as a dozen of The Firm's lawyers.

The Law Fibber

"I'm considering a number of offers from top firms."

Translation: I'm at the bottom of my class at The Jamaican School of Law.

The Overqualified

"I'll need a ten-thousand-dollar signing bonus, I won't do any of your crap work, I'll be a partner within five years, and I want my choice of a secretary."

The Slam Dunk

"Let's not waste both our time with your silly questions. You've probably noticed my last name is the same as that of The Firm's biggest client . . ."

▪ *The Rejection Letter: A Translation* ▪

An excellent source of Law Fibs is the standardized rejection letter The Firm sends to those applicants deemed unworthy of consideration. The key passages are translated below.

"Thank you for your interest in The Firm."
Translation: You sent your résumé to every place in town, didn't you?

"While your academic background, qualifications, and experience are very impressive . . ."
Translation: We didn't bother reading your résumé.

"Our current needs are not such that would allow us to grant you an interview at this time."
Translation: Bankruptcy is just around the corner for us and even if we were still viable, we've fired lots of lawyers much better than you.

"We will be sure to keep your résumé on file."
Translation: Your résumé is now being recycled into baby diapers.

"Good luck in your future endeavors."
Translation: Fuck off!

ATTORNEY EGOMETER

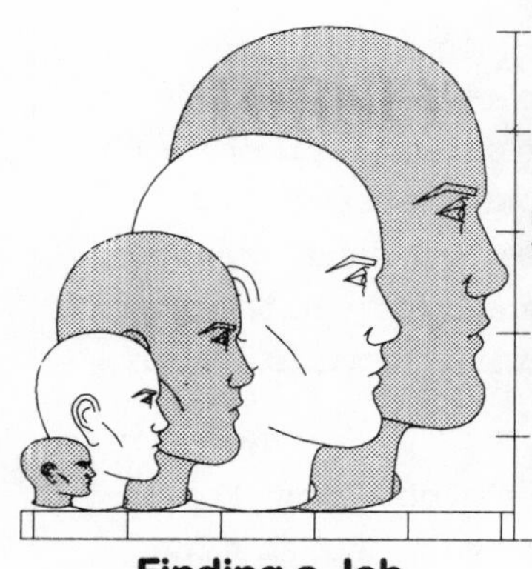

Finding a Job

THE FIRM

Internal Memorandum

TO: All Associates
FROM: The Recruiting Committee
RE: Interviewing Dos and Don'ts

In the near future, this year's batch of law students will begin visiting our office to interview for positions with The Firm. To avoid a repeat of last year's debacle (an out-of-court settlement is expected to be reached soon), we implore each of you to follow the guidelines described below when recruits are in the office.

Do appear friendly with other people from The Firm when in the presence of recruits. For instance, when you come upon another lawyer you've never even spoken to before, say something along the lines of: "Hey, great barbecue last weekend," "How about a drink after work?" or "Did I leave my shampoo in your shower?" **Warning:** Before doing so, be sure that the person you are addressing is not also a recruit. Said to the wrong people, these expressions could cause some confusion.

Don't berate subordinates in areas of the office where recruits might observe. If you are going to make someone cry, feel free to do so in a place where only Firm employees can watch.

Do pretend to enjoy your job if a recruit asks about The Firm's working environment. Law fib if you have to.

Don't ask recruits about their ethnic or family background, religion, marital status, or sexual preference. (These matters are now covered during the on-campus screening interview.)

Do be especially solicitous to those recruits with Roman numerals after their names.

▪ *Selecting a Firm* ▪

After interviews are completed, the recruit weighs job offers from various firms and then makes his selection. Aside from the primary consideration of salary, Prelawyers also consider the following factors in selecting a firm:

1. The propensity of the firm to generously settle wrongful termination lawsuits brought by disgruntled associates.

2. Prominent individuals in the legal community associated with the law firm. Having one or more of the following individuals on board can sway a recruit to choose a particular firm:

   - a highly visible partner who writes books used by law schools
   - a former partner who now serves as a judge
   - a lawyer who has litigated high-profile cases
   - a secretary who is also a cheerleader for the local professional football team
   - a recently-indicted partner prominent in the collapse of the savings and loan industry or other major public scandal

3. Location. This criteria is often overrated as associates rarely have an opportunity to leave the office. What is important is the number and quality of twenty-four-hour restaurants in the vicinity of The Firm since the young lawyer will dine most evenings at such establishments.

3

INSIDE THE MAZE: LAW FIRM LIFE

It's been a long hard road getting to The Firm, but once a lawyer arrives, life gets even more difficult. The carefree days (and free lunches) of the summer associate program are over. Things are different now that the associate is a full-time employee.

Instead of those fun and interesting projects of summers past, new lawyers are typically delegated to making copies, proofreading lengthy documents, running errands, and send-

Rodent's Firmiliar Quotations

The trouble with the law is lawyers.

—Clarence Darrow

The trouble with lawyers is law firms.

—The Rodent

The trouble with The Rodent is The Rodent.

—The Firm's Managing Partner

ing faxes for senior lawyers. Instead of being treated like favored guests, new associates now find themselves the Hated Rival to a score of The Firm's other lawyers who are out to ruin their careers.

In addition to the Hated Rival, each associate must now deal with many new enemies. These include untrustworthy staff, neglected spouses, rebellious kids, and, most importantly, partners.

Partners are the ones who carve up the profits and make the rules. At The Firm, the partner is the king, the master, the big wig, the top dog, the queen bee, the supreme and all powerful being. Associates, on the other hand, are the ones who do all the work and grind out the legal product for the financial benefit of partners. Associates are The Firm's slaves, gofers, indentured servants, pawns, hired hands, worker bees, and disposable proletariat.

Associates and partners are natural enemies.

It is a great irony of law firm life that while associates detest partners, at the same time they devote seven to ten

Rodent Tale

Steven Kumble from the now-defunct megafirm Finley, Kumble was obsessed with keeping lawyers in his firm from walking down the hallways without lids on their coffee cups. One afternoon, the president of the firm's client Kelley Oil Corporation, Joe Bridges, was using the office. Mr. Bridges was returning to a meeting after using the rest room when Kumble spotted him.

"Where the fuck is the top of your coffee cup?" Kumble yelled. "How many times do I have to tell you people! If I see you one more time in here without a lid on your cup, you are out of here—fired!"

Mr. Bridges froze in a state of shock as Kumble brushed past him. The client returned to the coffee room to get his lid, and there found Kumble slumped disconsolately in a chair in the corner.

"Let me introduce myself," Bridges said. "I'm the president of Kelley Oil Corporation."

"I'm sorry, I thought you worked here," said Kumble.

years of their lives trying to become one themselves. Despite these efforts, only a small percentage of associates survive to become partners in The Firm. Frequently, of an incoming class of as many as twenty or thirty associates, none are around long enough even to be considered for partnership.

Those few who succeed at The Firm do so by one of two methods. The first is through hard work and logging impressive numbers of hours that are billed to clients. The other road to partnership is developing business for The Firm. Without King Client, there's no work to do, no one to milk financially, and not enough revenue for each partner to buy a summer home. Lawyers who can bring a substantial amount of work into The Firm will thrive. This is because partners know these associates will take their clients with them if they are fired. The Firm simply can't afford to risk losing the business.

Onward to the next stage in the lawyer's career!

The Hated Rival

During law school orientation, new students are asked to look at the person sitting on their left and then the one on their right. One of the three of them, they are told, will fail to graduate. During orientation at The Firm, each associate should look at *all* of the other associates and know it's likely *none* of them will survive long enough to become a partner.

With such long odds, the associate must not only do everything possible to excel as an attorney but, at the same time, sabotage the careers of law firm peers. For this reason, at The Firm's orientation, each lawyer selects at least one other person whose career he or she will attempt to destroy. This person is fondly known as the Hated Rival.

There are a number of time-tested approaches lawyers use to hasten the demise of their Hated Rivals.

1. *Starting rumors of sexual impropriety.* The spreading of vicious false rumors about sexual relations between the Hated Rival and partners' bedmates is usually the

quickest and most effective way to hasten the Hated Rival's termination.

Warning: If the lawyer spreading the rumors happens to be married to the Hated Rival, this suggestion could backfire by reflecting poorly on the whole family. Care must also be taken not to link sexually the Hated Rival with someone who will help the Hated Rival's career, e.g., the senior partner.

2. *Tampering with the Hated Rival's documents.* While the complete deletion or destruction of important documents just before deadlines is quite effective in bringing down adversaries at The Firm, also recommended is adding language to documents likely to be sent to the client without the Hated Rival noticing. Revising tax provisions in documents that will cost the client millions or adding excerpts from children's books, quotations from *Penthouse* "Forum," or unflattering references to a partner's spouse in the middle of a document will usually do the trick.

3. *Whistle blowing.* Report to the state bar any number of instances of malpractice and unethical behavior (real or imagined) in which the Hated Rival partakes.

Lawyers should remember to always appear to be on friendly terms with the Hated Rival. This will not only help in playing other lawyers off each other but also make the attorney look less suspicious when the Hated Rival is fired and/or arrested.

Great Rivalries in Firm History

From The Firm's archives, here are some of the most effective ways to ruin a Hated Rival's career:

- Sneak into the Hated Rival's office on a Friday night, dial the continuous-playing weather report in Hong Kong, and then press the HOLD button.
- Send a copy of the résumé the Hated Rival gave to The Firm along with an accurate description of her background to the state bar.
- Send a letter under the Hated Rival's signature to all The Firm's clients. State that, due to its imminent collapse, The Firm will accept thirty cents on the dollar as full payment for all outstanding bills.
- Place an ad in the local legal newspaper saying The Firm will hire the first one hundred associates who show up at the Hated Rival's office on Monday morning.
- Send a bouquet of flowers and a sexually suggestive card to that partner at The Firm who has been harassing the Hated Rival.
- Send a letter, again under the Hated Rival's signature, to each of her clients. Admit to having a substance abuse problem and recommend that they find a new lawyer.

Rat Race Starting Line: The Associate Years

Among the names of lawyers on The Firm's letterhead is a small, apparently innocuous gap. While it may look insignificant, this gap is, in fact, the law firm equivalent of the Great Divide. It is the line separating the names of partners from those of associates.

Even the top recruits, from the top of their class at the top law schools, find themselves at the bottom when they begin work at The Firm. Life "below the line" is agonizingly difficult for every associate. All the sacrifice and pain associates endure is for purposes of making it above the line.

A few will climb above the line to enter the Promised Land of Partnership. Most, however, will slip along the way and their careers will tumble to their death.

Firm Personality Profile:
▪ *The Runaway Associate* ▪

Standing at The Firm: Partners used to really like her when she first started at The Firm because she billed incredible amounts of hours. She also seemed to be able to work forever without a break. Now, people are starting to worry about her mental health. (A dramatic deterioration in appearance and *physical* health is considered normal during a lawyer's first few years at The Firm.)

Social Life: Sometimes she takes a few minutes to speak with members of the cleaning crew who vacuum her office late at night.

Habits: Wearing the same clothes to the office two days in a row. (At other work places, this is a sign of sleeping over at someone else's place. At The Firm, it's a badge of courage and a sign of pulling an all-nighter.)

Secret Fantasy: To become The Firm's all-time Top Biller.

Future at The Firm: After working for seventy-two hours in a row, she cracks during a conference with a number of clients. She starts laughing uncontrollably for no reason, making animal noises and foaming at the mouth. Two weeks later, she is elected partner.

Firm Personality Profile:
▪ *The Runt Associate* ▪

Standing at The Firm: None really. Was hired only after the recruiting attorney's Hated Rival sent out an offer in place of a rejection letter. Most of The Firm's other lawyers aren't sure if he's a file clerk, a male secretary, or the Xerox man.

Social Life: Has secret crushes on most of The Firm's secretaries. Spends weekends at the office even when he has no work to do. All of the other lawyers seem to be busy for lunch and he ends up eating with paralegals and clerks who, because he outranks them, feel obligated to accept his invitation.

Hobbies: Race walking around the office trying to look really busy.

Secret Fantasy: To eat deli sandwiches late at night at the office with some of The Firm's really good lawyers.

Future at The Firm: Becomes the Runt Inmate (see Firm Fault Line, page 85).

Firm Personality Profile:
▪ *The Obsequious Associate* ▪

Standing at The Firm: Partners love him. Associates and staff despise him.

Habits: Lives at the office where he sleeps with *Black's Law Dictionary* (and anyone who can advance his career). Knows current billable hour tally of every attorney. Expert in dozens of legal fields.

Social Life: Has no real friends, only potential clients.

Hobbies: Memorizing names of each partner's spouse and kids. Sending birthday and holiday cards to everyone ranking above him at The Firm. Producing dog and pony shows for potential clients.

Secret Fantasy: It's no secret.

Favorite Movie: *Lawyers of Arabia*

Future at The Firm: In the natural evolution of lawyers, turns into the Runaway Associate.

▪ *Top Billing* ▪

Partners really don't care if their associates develop professionally and ably represent clients in court or in negotiations. In other words, most of those things typically said about The Firm when associates are interviewing for jobs are just big Law Fibs. What partners do care about is the associates profitability to The Firm.

With so much emphasis on the bottom line, an associate's professional performance is measured in quanitity (i.e., number of billable hours) rather than quality. Those associates who bill the most hours see their stock at The Firm soar and are amply rewarded. Meanwhile, those who lag behind in the Billable Hours Derby suffer the consequences.

Top Biller

1. Given choice, partner-sized office with beautiful view.
2. Enjoys friendly attention from partners who invite Top Biller for drinks at The Club.
3. Has The Firm's best secretary.
4. Put on exciting assignments and sent to meetings in resort locations. Commonly commits malpractice but no one seems to care.
5. Is The Firm's Star Associate and treated like a celebrity —almost like a partner.

Low Biller

1. Shares windowless office with Runt Associate.
2. Invited to pour drinks for partners and Top Biller.
3. Still trying to get a replacement for the secretary who left months ago. Does own typing and answers own phone (on those rare occasions when it rings).
4. Serves as The Firm's stop-and-fetch boy. Sent to make deliveries when the courier service is running behind schedule. Also does a lot of proofreading of other lawyer's documents.
5. Will never amount to anything.

▪ *Associate Egometer* ▪

The associate's life is a continuous drop in self-esteem as partners trash the attorney for poor work product, insufficient billable hours, and substandard legal skills. This is part of the ride that begins on the first day of work and ends in the inevitable termination that lies "at the end of the Egometer."

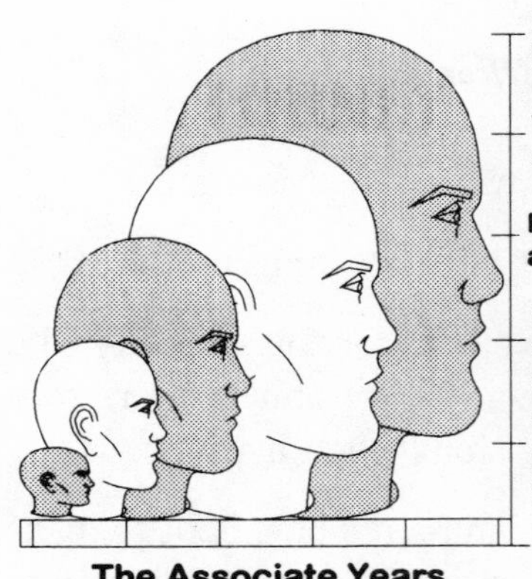

The Associate Years

The Partnership Track

The goal of every associate is to become a partner at The Firm. Those who claim otherwise are either law fibbing or merely making a thinly veiled attempt to protect their standing on the Egometer. With so few surviving long enough even to be considered for election, everything the lawyer does must be calculated to take her to the Promised Land of Partnership.

Many of the associate's actions will reflect favorably among the partners who make the decision about her future, while other events may hurt her chances. In either case, everything the associate does is observed and evaluated. One false move and the associate can be knocked off the Partnership Track and lose the Game.

Rodent Tale

Only one of ten associates who started at New York's thirty largest firms in the early 1980s were among the partnership ranks a decade later. The Partnership Track at most firms is between seven and nine years.

One firm, Cadwalader, Wickersham & Taft, promoted the smallest percentage, just one associate out of eighty-three (1.2 percent). The firm Shea & Gould elevated the highest percentage among firms in the survey, thirteen out of sixty (21.6 percent). Shea & Gould is now defunct.

PART

COLLECTIONS

GO STRAIGHT TO HELL	7 Steps Back	2 Steps Back	3 Steps Back	1 Step Back	1 Step Forward	8 Steps Forward	1 Step Back	2 Steps Forward	GRADUATE FROM LAW SCHOOL ROLL DICE
	State Bar Requires Firm to Verify All Attorneys' Bar Numbers.	Hated Rival Uses Heimlich Maneuver to Save Your Life at Firm Picnic.	FBI Sets Fire to Your Compound.	Caught in Compromising Position with Summer Associate.	Caught in Compromising Position with Sr. Partner.	You Catch Sr. Partner in Compromising Position with Summer Associate.	Accidentally Leave On-line Computer Program on All Weekend.	Client Pays Computer Bill. Firm Finds New Revenue Source.	

1 Step Back	3 Steps Forward	2 Steps Back	Steps Forward
Stabbed in Back While Playing Tennis.	The Firm Also Represents Exxon.	Miss Filing Deadline for Exxon Valdez Pro Bono Case on Behalf of Environmentalists.	Lie on Witness Stand to Keep Partner from Going to Jail.

2 Steps Forward	2 Steps Back	2 Steps Forward	3 Steps Back
Bring in Major Client.	Your Major Client Fails to Pay Bill.	Wife Gives Birth to Baby.	You Give Birth to Baby.

CORNER OFFICE

1 Step Back — Whacked on Knee Just Before You're Voted on for Partnership.

3 Steps Back — Johnnie Cochran Named Co-counsel. Steals Your Spotlight.

2 Steps Back — Firm Gets Bad Press for Having No Minority Partners.

3 Steps B[…] — Morn[…] Tem[…] Veri[…] You're Eski[…]

Rules: None.

Goal: To outlive other associates.

Prize: Six figure income, divorce, triple bypass, resentment of colleagues and children, joint and several liability for malpractice suits.

[…]RSHIP

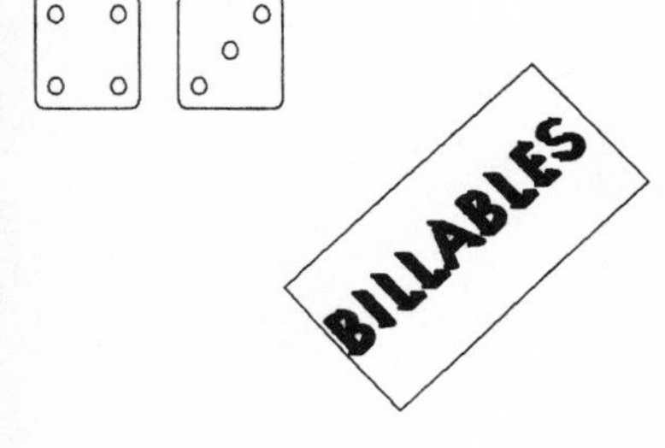

5 Steps Forward — You Destroy All Documents and Beat Rap.

2 Steps Back — RICO Indictment for Aiding and Abetting Client.

3 Steps Back — Husband Refuses to Appoint You to Supreme Court.

5 Steps Forward — Husband Elected President.

2 Steps Forward — Husband Elected Governor.

1 Step Forward — Bill 3,400 Hours in One Fiscal Year.

2 Steps Forward — Hated Rival Mysteriously Poisoned at Firm Dinner.

3 Steps Back — Hated Rival Becomes Partner.

OF COUNSEL

[…] Forward	2 Steps Forward	2 Steps Back	2 Steps Back
[…]d Test […]s Senior […]tner Is […]s Father.	Draft a 120 Page Contract in One Night.	Take a One Week Vacation.	Caught Reading This Book in Your Office.

Firm Fashion

Lawyers are, by law, required to wear the same basic uniform to The Firm. The only variations on the standard dress code derive from the various stages of a lawyer's career.

Women

First-Year Associate— The "This is the first time I've ever worn heels" look.

Senior Associate— The "We can have a baby just as soon as I'm elected partner, dear" look.

Senior Partner— The "I stopped caring about my appearance when my annual income first exceeded a quarter of a million dollars" look.

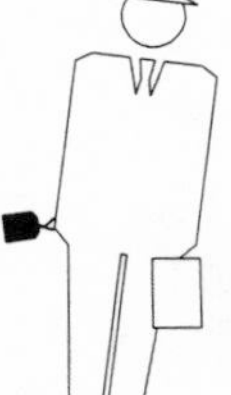

Men

First-Year Associate— The "I bought this suit my junior year of college and it still almost fits" look.

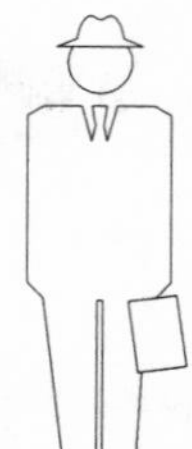

Senior Associate— The "I've worked for seventy-two straight hours"Runaway Associate look.

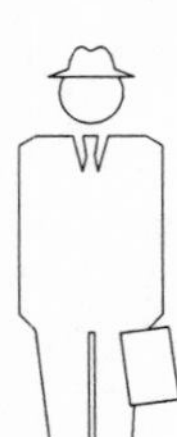

Senior Partner— The "My wife died and now I have to try to take care of myself" look.

Rodent Tale

"You can change the houses but the contents of the closets are always the same," fashion consultant Charmaine McClarie-Cox says of attorneys' wardrobes.

"Wool suits in navy blue or gray, one remnant from the polyester-blend era, white button-down shirts, neckties with little-bitty diamonds or polka dots or stars, elasticized suspenders and several pairs of wingtips," says Ms. McClarie-Cox. "It's a look that says, 'I'm stuck, I'm boring, I'm not open to change, I'm afraid to stand out, I've been wearing this since I left Harvard or Yale.' "

Ms. McClarie-Cox says that the woman lawyers who come to her tend to look "androgynous" and "unkempt." She advises younger lawyers that the macho, masochistic look is out. It used to be a sign to superiors that they were sufficiently self-sacrificing. Now, "a crisp, pulled-together looks says, 'I'm confident and ready to take on more.' "

Rodent Tale

The Los Angeles law firm Latham & Watkins was sued by a client for alleged overbilling. The client offered as an exhibit a photograph of several of the firm's paralegals dressed in T-shirts that read "Born to Bill." The client claimed that this symbolized the firm's mentality and its "scorched-earth" policy designed to generate high legal fees while preparing cases for trial.

Law Firm Maladies

After a few weeks at The Firm, the first-year associate begins to feel the effects of practicing law. Most lawyers suffer from a number of specific illnesses, unique to The Firm's environment, known as "Law Firm Maladies."

Pre-Filing Phobia (PFP). Inability to stray more than five feet from your secretary while she is preparing pleadings that have to be filed by the end of the day.

ASAP Anxiety. Partial paralysis due to ringing telephones and paging on The Firm's intercom.

Post-Closing Syndrome (PCS). Temporary feeling of euphoria followed by extreme sense of uselessness after completing a major transaction.

Partner Paranoia. Fear of answering interoffice phone calls and venturing into hallways, rest rooms, elevators, and other places where partners lurk.

Anal Retention Affliction (ARA). Obsession with proper spelling and grammar. Victims are primarily transactional attorneys.

Attorney Attendants

People working at The Firm are divided into two basic categories—the haves and the have-nots. What law firm personnel either have or don't have is a law degree.

While the dividing line between partners and associates is very clear, it pales in comparison to the one between lawyers and members of the staff. Aside from clandestine sexual relations, there is virtually no social interaction between the juris doctored and their subordinates. Thus, while it is perfectly acceptable law firm behavior for a lawyer to be caught naked with a member of the staff in The Firm's supply room, an attorney wouldn't be caught dead having lunch or drinks with that same staffer (fully clothed).

Although commonly used and abused by lawyers, the nameless and faceless paralegals, secretaries, mail room personnel, and others from The Firm's cast of characters do, on occasion, get the upper hand. There are times, in fact, when members of the staff can virtually make or break a lawyer. On these occasions, roles are reversed, tables are turned, and unless the staffers go on to become lawyers themselves, these moments become the highlights of their careers.

▪ *The Legal Secretary* ▪

While few lawyers would ever admit it, legal secretaries are generally highly committed, professional, and skilled individuals who know more about the law than many attorneys. The fact that secretaries are used and abused by lawyers and rarely acknowledged for their skills and hard work is, well, just their tough luck for not going to law school themselves.

Good lawyers know the important role secretaries play. Whenever the lawyer screws up and is called to the mat by a senior attorney, a client, or an investigator from the state bar, lawyers turn to their secretary for help.

- Oversleep and miss a deadline, appointment, or court appearance? Your secretary forgot to put it on your calendar.
- Make a mistake in drafting a document that cost the client millions? Your secretary made a typo.
- Forget your spouse's birthday? Your secretary forgot to buy a present.

- Your spouse is complaining about your late hours? You're having an affair with your secretary.
- Famine in Africa? Your secretary caused adverse weather patterns for the Southern Hemisphere.

Firm Personality Profile:
▪ *The Senior Executive Secretary* ▪

Disposition: Sweet as honey to partners and anyone who has been at The Firm over ten years. Queen of the bitches to everyone else.

Social Life: Lives alone since bludgeoning her kitten to death.

Standing at The Firm: Joined The Firm when it opened as a three-person outfit forty years ago. Former mistress to senior partner and holds that over his head. Has the run of The Firm.

Hobbies: Reading, bird watching, needlepoint, ruining the careers of young female attorneys.

Greatest Achievement: Solely responsible for the firing of three office managers in a two-month period.

Secret Fantasy: To kill that first-year punk associate she is forced to work for.

Rodent Tale

The California Supreme Court accepted the resignation of Attorney Burke Burford after receiving a letter in which he admitted stealing money from his clients. Another one of Attorney Burford's problems was that he didn't learn of his own resignation until one month later when a friend called to ask him about it.

It seems that after Attorney Burford's secretary stole $268,000 from his client's trust accounts, she kept state bar investigators at bay as long as she could by intercepting their phone calls and turning them away at the office door. Eventually, the secretary told the bar that her boss was aware of the investigation and intended to resign. The resignation letter was then sent to the state bar. All of this without the knowledge of Attorney Burford. "That's what I got for being so confident in my secretary's abilities," he said.

Secretarial Law Fibs

"The system is down."

Translation: I don't feel like working right now. Go away!

"I'm going to report you to the client/the state bar/the FBI/your spouse."
Translation: I want a raise.

"No, I'm sorry, he is in court/at a closing/at the state bar convention/ on another call/in intensive care/ now with the Clinton Administration."
Translation: He is going to be about a week late with that document you're waiting for.

"The White-Out doesn't seem to work on this computer screen."

or

"The fax machine is broken—the paper keeps coming out the other end instead of going to the person I'm trying to send it to."
Translation: I was hired because I'm beautiful. You better find someone else to do your work.

"Those suspenders and matching tie really look great!"
Translation: Did your wife die?

Firm Personality Profile:
▪ *The Evil Office Manager* ▪

Disposition: When you first meet her, she appears to be the nicest and friendliest person you've ever encountered. About a month later, you come to realize she is extremely nasty and petty.

Social Life: A total and complicated mess. You don't even want to hear about it. But you will.

Standing at The Firm: Despite being the most hated person at The Firm (especially by the secretaries), everyone's very nice to her. This is because she decides which secretary works with which lawyer, and who gets the good office furniture and supplies. (You'd be amazed to learn what attorneys are willing to do for a brand new dictaphone.)

Hobbies: Firing secretaries who are five minutes late or who are guilty of minor violations of The Firm's dress code.

Future at The Firm: Eventually fired after being undermined by the Senior Executive Secretary. She sues The Firm for wrongful termination. When The Firm's own lawyers appear in court to defend themselves, the jury sympathizes with her and awards her millions.

Firm Personality Profile:
▪ The Mail Guy ▪

Disposition:
Seems to be the happiest and friendliest person in the office but, as everyone finds out later, has a very dark side and is deeply troubled.

Social Life: Sexually hyperactive, having affairs with numerous people at The Firm.

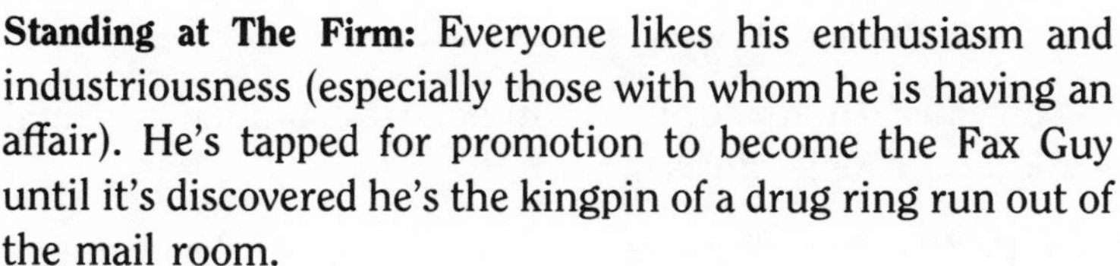

Standing at The Firm: Everyone likes his enthusiasm and industriousness (especially those with whom he is having an affair). He's tapped for promotion to become the Fax Guy until it's discovered he's the kingpin of a drug ring run out of the mail room.

Proudest Achievement: Retaliation against a senior associate who was mean to him. He intentionally misdirected a confidential memorandum from the client to opposing counsel. The lawyer was sued for malpractice and fired.

Hobbies: Opening and reading other people's personal mail.

Future at The Firm: Caught stealing office equipment but not fired because he knows too much from reading everyone's mail.

Secret Fantasy: He's living it.

Firm Personality Profile:
▪ *The Party Girl Paralegal* ▪

Personal Life: None, her whole life is at The Firm. Has already found two of her previous husbands there.

Legal Skills: Dramatically declining. Hasn't done any real work for a couple of years.

Favorite Pastimes: Stopping by other people's office to chat, waiting for five o'clock to come around, so she can get a group of people from the office to go out for drinks. Also enjoys telling new lawyers who don't know any better that she will do the work they ask her to do.

Career Highlight: Having interoffice intercourse with two partners in the same day.

Professional Reputation: She has quite a reputation, but it's not for her paralegal skills. Everyone knows that no matter how incompetent and inefficient she is, she will never be fired. The firm needs her!

Rodent Tale

The Los Angeles law firm Latham & Watkins is credited with starting a trend by placing members of the staff in office space separate from that occupied by the firm's attorneys.

When partners and associates moved into the beautiful new First Interstate World Center in downtown Los Angeles, the firm's administrative offices, litigation support, and accounting, finance, and data processing departments were housed in a more modest building a block away. Besides the view and the different degrees of plushness, the two buildings distinguished themselves from each other by twenty-five dollars a square foot.

While some might fear that isolating the staff in more modest surroundings reinforces the class divisions between lawyers and staff, this is not necessarily such a bad thing from the perspective of members of the staff. Said one employee of another firm utilizing the back office approach: "The support staff is going to have a lot of fun in their own building—because there will be no attorneys there."

Shopping for the Staff

Lawyers generally don't care about anyone ranking below them at The Firm. At the same time, they know the importance of manipulating people of all levels in order to advance their own careers. For the holidays and birthdays, lawyers at The Firm therefore purchase gifts for members of the staff and other colleagues as a token of their feigned appreciation.

For the Mail Guy: A "Get Out of Jail Free" card.

For That Special Paralegal Who Always Bails Out the Lawyer by Staying Late and Taking the Blame for the Lawyer's Mistakes: Nothing. Lawyers have to show who's boss.

For the Secretary: Secretaries also need to be shown who's boss but failing to give presents encourages nasty lunchroom stories about the lawyer. One gift idea is that computer screen the overworked secretary has been trying to get ever since she started developing cataracts.

For the Paralegal Party Girl: Her very own key to The Firm's supply room.

For the Hated Rival: Something really nice and expensive (so she won't suspect you).

For Family and Friends: Firm monogrammed pencils, pens, and legal pads stolen from The Firm's supply room.

For Partners: Anything really cheap (under ten dollars) and so embarrassing that the recipient will feel uncomfortable even mentioning the gift. Send the gifts to each partner along with an affectionate card from your Hated Rival.

▪ *The Staff Conspiracy* ▪

Many lawyers think it's just their bad luck when everything seems to go wrong. These same lawyers are often under the impression that members of The Firm's staff are powerless. Those who have had their careers ruined by a Staff Conspiracy know better.

Staff Conspiracies are enacted from time to time to retaliate against overly arrogant and abusive lawyers. They are often put into action when such lawyers find themselves up against an important and urgent deadline.

Abusive Attorney receives phone call from Client or Partner giving instructions to drop everything and take on a crucial project that must be completed immediately. It is made clear that the Abusive Attorney's career depends on this assignment.

▼

After learning of Abusive Attorney's assignment by eavesdropping on the phone conversation, Secretary calls Paralegal and explains the situation. Paralegal informs other paralegals so each of them can stand ready to tell Abusive Attorney they are too busy to help with the project.

▼

Paralegal calls Librarian, who hides all The Firm's research material Abusive Attorney needs to complete the urgent project.

▼

Librarian calls Fax Operator and warns him Abusive Attorney will soon need to transmit some urgent documents. Fax Operator causes all fax machines to go on the fritz. As a backup, Mail Guy calls pal in Memphis who works at the Federal Express headquarters. Mail Guy requests that any packages sent by Abusive Attorney be misdirected to overseas destinations.

▼

Xerox Man is alerted. He arranges for all copying machines and printers to run out of toner simultaneously.

▼

Xerox Man contacts Word Processing Department. The head operator causes The Firm's computer system to crash.

▼

Staff member with whom Abusive Attorney is sleeping shows up at office crying and threatening to disclose the liaison unless they talk over their entire relationship *immediately*.

▼

Conspirators alert Abusive Attorney's Hated Rival, who, with full cooperation of the staff, completes the assignment. When the deadline passes and Abusive Attorney has to confess to failing to complete the project, Hated Rival gives finalized work product to Client or Partner.

▼

Abusive Attorney is fired. The staff celebrates and selects Hated Rival as their next target.

The Firm Fault Line

1. Client makes frantic call to The Firm: "Federal authorities are here telling me I'm going to jail for thirty years. That memo you sent me said it was okay to dump our toxic waste in the community swimming pool!"

2. Partner, who doesn't remember the memo or the advice, tells Client that "my associate must have made a mistake with the research." Partner calls Associate to tell her of the embarrassing development and vows to have her fired.

3. Associate, not knowing what Partner is talking about, tells Partner she relied on data supplied to her by Paralegal to reach the conclusions in the memo.

4. Paralegal, who was never involved in this project but who knows how things work at The Firm, claims Secretary sent Associate erroneous information.

5. Secretary, who was fired from her last job because she was the last person on the Fault Line, is prepared this time and blames Mail Guy for delivering the wrong documents to Associate.

6. Mail Guy claims he was simply following instructions given to him by Runt Associate.

7. Runt Associate, who hadn't even started working at The Firm when the memo was sent to Client, takes full responsibility for the bad advice. He does Client's prison time and is badly mistreated by other inmates.

Law Firm Emergency Response Plan

Should a natural disaster or other catastrophe strike The Firm while the office is occupied, all personnel are advised to follow the procedures described below.

1. *Listen for instructions.* Immediately following a catastrophe, a prerecorded message from the Senior Partner will be played over the office intercom and on the voice mail system. The message will assure personnel:
   a. The building is safe and those inside should continue working. This will save thousands of billable hours as it could take days before city officials declare the building uninhabitable.
   b. Anyone leaving the office or failing to report to work will be fired. To those who have never worked in a law firm, this may seem a bit insensitive. Experience has shown, however, that it's far easier to abandon injured and distressed loved ones when the Senior Partner insists upon it.

2. *Know the safety routes.* Elevators and main entrances are likely to be blocked, which can hinder those trying to get to work. Familiarize yourself with emergency exits that can be used to get *into* the office at the time of the disaster. Unchecked freight elevators and stairways should be identified. While walking the fifty flights of stairs to the office, personnel are reminded not to panic and to climb at a normal pace.

3. *Activate alternative energy sources.* Backup electrical generators should be activated to keep the word processing terminals operative. Flashlights are stored in the library so that legal research will not be interrupted.

4. *Keep phone lines free.* Telephone lines must be kept open for faxes and calls from new clients seeking emergency counsel. Those ranking below partner are forbidden to use telephones to check on the safety of loved ones. Just assume everyone's okay. Family and friends should also be instructed not to call into The Firm, unless, of course, they are in need of emergency legal counsel.

5. *Follow the evacuation plan.* If it is *absolutely* certain that the building is going to either collapse or burn to the ground, evacuate in the following order:
   a. Partners
   b. Associates (according to billable hour rate)
   c. Of Counsel
   d. Secretaries
   e. Office manager
   f. Other staff
   (Note: It is a law firm tradition that paralegals go down with The Firm.)

6. *Abandon personal possessions.* In case of evacuation, all law firm personnel should take only their time sheets with them and leave other personal possessions and colleagues behind. Remember, The Firm can bill for replacing files lost in the emergency.

7. *Stock emergency rations.* Store sufficient drinking water and nonperishable food (charged to the client) to assure survival for up to a month at the office with no contact from the outside world. (Most associates are already familiar with this practice.)

8. *Attend emergency informative meeting.* Immediately following the emergency, the Construction Law and Insurance Claims Practice Group will meet in the main conference room. All attorneys are required to report for further instructions concerning The Firm's plan for making the most out of the calamity and drumming up new business.

4

Running Up the Clock

Lawyers sell their time and the price of their time is generally based on the individual lawyer's experience. While lawyers just starting at The Firm are billed to clients in the neighborhood of between $100 and $150 an hour, rates for some partners can run as high as $500 an hour. Some celebrity attorneys charge even more!

Although it's hard to imagine what any one person could possibly do for another person that would be worth $500 an

Rodent's Firmiliar Quotations

Extremism in overbilling is no vice. And moderation in calculating client expense reimbursements is no virtue.

—Firm motto

hour, the rates charged by lawyers at The Firm just aren't enough. Hourly billing rates are supplemented by "the pad"—the lawyer's way of keeping time that exaggerates the number of minutes spent on behalf of a client. Another trick of the time trade is to put more lawyers on a job than are necessary to complete it. Also helpful are the surcharges added to the various office functions necessary for lawyers to get the job done. Everything from phone calls to faxes and air-conditioning are targets of The Firm's surcharge.

Like auto mechanics who charge innocent motorists for all sorts of illusory engine problems, lawyers run up clients' bills by completing projects that are unnecessary. The only difference is that with a car, you might get your tires unnecessarily rotated. At The Firm, you might have your case taken all the way to the U.S. Supreme Court.

Time Bandits

Like psychotherapists, plumbers, and some prostitutes, lawyers charge by the hour. A typical lawyer's hour, however, is much longer than sixty minutes.

To make things more profitable, lawyers bill in six-, fifteen-, or twenty-minute increments, depending on the firm. A two-hundred-dollar-an-hour lawyer billing in fifteen-minute increments, for example, charges clients at least fifty dollars (not including pad) for everything he does, no matter how small and insignificant. This turns short, effortless events into big profits for The Firm. A collection of these small tasks (especially when combined with the pad) can stretch an hour out to infinity.

Firm Personality Profile:
▪ *The Billing Champion* ▪

Legal Background: Back-to-back annual Top Biller and has the chance to be the first associate in The Firm's history to three-peat.

Personal Life: None since husband left her for a government lawyer who works nine to five. Spends most nights sleeping on office couch. Would like to remarry because she misses having someone to run errands for her.

Hobbies: Squeezing more than twenty-four billable hours into one day.

Greatest Achievement: Once worked on a transaction in Tokyo and continued billing on the flight home. Taking advantage of the time zones, she logged thirty-two billable hours in one day.

Future at The Firm: Elected partner posthumously.

Favorites: Movie: *Time Bandits.* Television show: *Beat the Clock.* Book: *The Time Machine.* Magazine: *Time.* Song: "Eight Days a Week."

▪ *Time Sheets and the Pad* ▪

(When Twenty-four Hours a Day Just Isn't Enough!)

Perhaps the most crucial aspect of the practice of law is the completion of time sheets. Lawyers at The Firm use time sheets to keep track of what they do on behalf of clients. Each time sheet entry is eventually turned into a bill that is sent to a client.

Time sheets tell partners how much attorneys at The Firm are producing and thus determine their worth as a lawyer (and as a person). Exceeding The Firm's annual billable hours is absolutely essential in order to be elected to partnership.

This situation places tremendous pressure on lawyers to inflate the amount of time they spend on each matter. This practice is known as "padding" hours and is often the only way lawyers can achieve the 1,900 or 2,000 hours The Firm expects them to bill each year.

In the good old days, The Firm used to get away with submitting bills to clients that simply stated the amount due for "services rendered." Today, clients demand more detailed accounts of The Firm's work.

As the following time sheet and corresponding description of what actually occurs demonstrate, clients still know very little about what they are paying for.

Rodent Tale

One Texas law firm set billing goals of 6,000 hours a year for attorneys (at most firms, annual goals range between 1,800 and 2,100 hours). That works out to 115 hours a week, or 23 hours a day. Secretaries at the firm were instructed to bill the time of attorneys even when they were away on vacation.

▪ *The Firm Time Sheet* ▪

Day 1. Client calls Partner to ask for copy of her company's corporate bylaws. Partner on phone with bookie, Secretary takes message.

Phone conference with Client. 0.5 Hour ($150).

Day 4. Client calls again. Partner at the ballpark with other clients.

Phone conference with Client, research re new developments in corporate law. Review of tax code. 2.5 Hours ($750).

Day 12. After six more unsuccessful calls to Partner, Client calls Associate who drafted bylaws. Associate calls the Paralegal and asks her to find them. Paralegal tells Secretary to find bylaws. Because Partner is "working at home," Secretary calls Partner to ask if he knows where she can find the bylaws. Partner chastises Secretary for calling him at home.

Associate: Review and revise bylaws. 1 Hour ($200). Paralegal: Review and revise bylaws. 1 Hour ($140). Partner: Review and revise bylaws. 2 Hours ($600).

Day 17. Client runs into Partner on the golf course, tells him she spoke with Associate. Client asks Partner when she can expect bylaws. Partner, not knowing what Client is talking about, says, "The bylaws are in the mail."

Partner: Conference with Client re status of file. Meeting with partners re firing of Associate for talking to Client without permission. 3.5 Hours ($1,050). Associate: Interoffice conference re status of file. Reproduction of files and compilation of evidence for defending Associate's wrongful termination suit. 15 Hours ($3,000).

Days 19–28. After Client calls again begging for help, Partner asks Associate if he knows where bylaws are. Associate says he sent them to the file room via interoffice mail. Mail Guy runs a tracer and informs Partner the bylaws should arrive in file room in four to six more business days. When bylaws are located, Partner's Secretary sends them to Client's Singapore office.

Phone conference with Client re corporate structure and related bylaws. Conference with Associate re same. Research re possible violations of Securities and Exchange Act and potential protection for Client by incorporating under laws of the State of Delaware. 3.5 Hours ($1,050).

Day 29. Client calls to tell Partner she urgently needs bylaws to give to Bank as part of a major loan the company is seeking. Partner on the phone with his travel agent. Tells Secretary to tell Client he will get back to her later in the week.

Research re domestic and international traveler's check law. 4 Hours ($1,500).

Day 31. Deadline passes. Loan lost. Secretary explains situation to Partner, who chastises her for not calling him at home. To retrieve the bylaws, Partner has Secretary book flight to Singapore. Takes The Firm's new paralegal with him. Partner and Paralegal arrive in Singapore, but Client's office is closed due to failed financing back in the States. Partner and Paralegal fly to Bali for the weekend.

Partner: Travel to Singapore. 15 Hours ($4,500). Paralegal: Travel. 13 Hours ($1,300). Travel expenses ($10,000).

Day 38. Partner runs into Client at the theater and tells her she should "sue those bastards at the Bank." The Firm will handle the case.

Conference with Client and related research. 5 Hours ($1,500).

Days 116–118. The day before the filing is due, Partner asks First-Year Associate to draft complaint against Bank. Associate responds by explaining she is on her way out the door because she is getting married the next day. Partner convinces Associate the project "will only take a few hours." Associate makes it to wedding but skips reception and honeymoon to get back to the office.

Associate: Drafting of pleadings against Bank and research re sexual harassment claim filed by Paralegal resulting out of the trip to Bali with Partner. 30 Hours ($4,500).

Day 119. Bank's counsel agrees to meet to discuss settling case. Partner goes to meeting and finds another one of The Firm's partners there representing Bank. The partners laugh, go for drinks, and decide it wouldn't be in either of

Rodent Tale

A partner at a California law firm admitted to a court that he required billing clerks to follow a schedule he devised that added specific amounts of time to those billed by attorneys. He testified that this was done not to defraud clients but to "recapture" billable hours he believed attorneys forgot to charge to clients. The court estimated that the firm had overcharged clients by as much as $1 million by applying the recovered memory technique to billing.

their interest to settle case until *after* it has been tried. They agree to arm wrestle to see who gets to win the case.

Interoffice conference re status of case. Attend settlement conference. 4 Hours ($1,200).
Refreshments: ($170).

Day 120. Hated Rival deletes and destroys all of Associate's work on pleading that is due today. Associate finds a different pleading for a personal injury case in another lawyer's office, changes the names and leaves draft on Partner's desk for his review.

Tax research. 10 Hours ($3,000). Damages paid to Paralegal for sexual harassment claim ($215,000).

Day 121. Associate tells Partner she filed pleading at the wrong court house.

Associate: Prepare and argue motion in court. 15

Rodent Tale

Because clients cannot be billed until The Firm has collected and processed its time sheets, lawyers at The Firm are constantly pestered to get their time sheets completed on time. It is a common scene at any law firm to see the managing partner making the rounds to remind other lawyers to complete their time sheets and send them to the accounting department.

One managing partner remembers encountering a fellow partner who, at the time, was having marital problems and suffering from various physical disorders. The managing partner walked into the other partner's office and discovered him lying on the floor writhing in pain, holding his hand on his back near his left kidney. "I am never good in those situations," the partner recounts, "I never know what to say or do. So, I said the first thing that came into my mind: 'Howard, are your time sheets in?' "

Hours ($3,000). Partner: Attend strategy session. 2 Hours ($600).

Day 122. Partner calls Client and tells her: "The law isn't on our side on this one," advises conceding the case to avoid adverse publicity.

Conference with Client re status of case. 1 Hour ($300).

Day 141. In the mail, Client receives bylaws forwarded from Singapore and The Firm's bill for **$253,510.**

Surcharge It!

Lawyers at The Firm are skillful in identifying seemingly innocuous office items and turning them into revenue sources. To a nonlawyer, the fax and Xerox machines, for example, might look like simple office equipment. When The Firm's surcharges are added in, however, these devices become huge law firm money-makers and produce enough revenue to send the partners' kids to Ivy League law schools. Added to everything from postage to pastries, the surcharge is The Firm's financial lifeblood.

Rodent Tale

In a 1991 article in *The American Lawyer* a new legal phrase was coined to describe law firm surcharges placed on office services. The term is "Skaddenomics," from the article of the same name describing the billing practices of the firm Skadden, Arps, Slate, Meagher & Flom.

Of the many items that Skadden, Arps charged to its clients, the most interesting are the now-famous pastries. The pastries came to the nation's attention when a senior associate ordered coffee, juice, and Danish for four from Skadden, Arps's in-house cafeteria at the firm's Washington, D.C., office. The associate indicated on the order that the items be charged to the account of a client.

On the order form completed by the cafeteria, the price of the items was listed at $23.80. The charge was rounded to $24 and then, in handwritten notes on the order form, increased by forty percent. The client was billed $33.60 for the Danish and beverages without being informed of the markup. Other charges made to the same client by the firm that at the same time was charging between $135 and $300 per hour for attorney time included:

- $42,386 for meals eaten by Skadden lawyers and staff. While most of those working late ate at the office, one associate on the case regularly treated himself to dinners at a local restaurant costing between $30 and $40.

- A series of charges (under $5,000 each) for staff and litigation support, copy service staff ($35 an hour), courier service (almost always by Skadden employees), library staff ($45 an hour) and proofreaders.

- $1,490 for a computer service used to do legal research plus a twenty-five percent markup).

- $17 for a courier to deliver a seventy-five-cent newspaper.

Although the firm eventually cut $1.1 million off the bill, a Skadden partner questioned about these items responded: "We have determined that our statements for services rendered and costs and expenses incurred were generated in accordance with normal billing practices." Another partner said this particular client was unaccustomed to the types of charges typically billed by big-city firms. In fact, he said, the firm charged the client less than it would have billed other clients.

T H E F I R M

Internal Memorandum

TO: All Attorneys and Paralegals
FROM: The Accounting Department
RE: Copying Charges

As some of you are aware, a major accounting firm was recently challenged by a client over the sixty-seven cents per page the accounting firm charges for copying services. This is of great concern to us as it has always been The Firm's policy to charge seventy cents per page plus the usual $125 per hour for the junior associate making the copies. This combination has made the photocopy room a major profit center for The Firm over the past several years. In fact, just one Xerox machine generated more revenue last fiscal year than did the entire Wills & Trusts Practice Group.

We are, of course, concerned that our own clients will get wind of this development. As a preemptive move, we have reduced our charges to fifty cents per page. To compensate for the resulting loss in revenue, we encourage all attorneys and paralegals to more actively use office services in order to run up surcharges.

Specifically, we suggest making at least two extra copies of each document we reproduce, making longer and more frequent long distance phone calls (including personal calls that we traditionally charge to our bigger clients), and eating more pastries served at office meetings.

Rodent Tale

There are 744 hours in a 31-day month. Don't tell that to Attorney Mark Kirby of Raleigh, North Carolina, who billed over 1,200 hours in a single month. It was reported that Attorney Kirby's goal was to be the richest lawyer in Wake County (i.e., earn as much as a second-year associate at a major New York firm.)

A spokesman for the North Carolina Bar Association reacted to the news of Kirby's billing practices by saying, "We would be concerned if lawyers bill more hours than exist in a day."

The United States attorney trying the case brought against Kirby for overbilling said in his closing arguments that hours are hours—billable or otherwise. Attorney Kirby's lawyer countered this argument by saying that the standard clock is simply not applicable to a lawyer's billable workday.

The jury deadlocked on the case.

▪ *The Surcharge: A Case Study* ▪

A lawyer, working out of the Miami office of a New York-based law firm, is on a case requiring her to travel to Chicago. Upon arrival, the lawyer realizes she needs a copy of a hundred-page document she left behind at the Miami office. From Chicago the next morning, the laywer prepares a fax to her secretary requesting she be sent the document. The secretary calls the laywer to confirm.

Actual Cost to The Firm

FAX: Toll call = $1.00

COPYING: $0.02 per page = $2.00

FEDERAL EXPRESS = $7.50 (corporate rate)

PHONE CALL = $3.00

ATTORNEY TIME (*all resulting from the lawyer forgetting document*): 15 minutes (at $300 an hour) = $75.00

BREAKFAST PASTRIES AND COFFEE = $6.50

TRAVEL = $425.00

HOTEL = $145.00

Total: $665.00

What the Client Is Billed

FAX: $3.00 per page plus double toll = $8.00

COPYING: $0.50 per page (two extra file copies) = $150.00

FEDERAL EXPRESS: (*100% surcharge*) plus secretarial overtime in preparing = $50.00

PHONE CALL (plus personal calls) = $56.00

BILLABLE HOURS: 15 minutes (plus pad = one hour) = $300.00

BREAKFAST PASTRIES AND COFFEE: $17.00 (plus one billable hour to eat) = $317.00

TRAVEL: First class: $1,650.00 Billable time spent sleeping plus phone calls to friends from air phone ($1.75 a minute) = $120.00

HOTEL: Presidential Suite: $475.00

EXTRAS: Chicago is colder than Miami and that poplin suit isn't heavy enough. New suit = $600.00

ENTERTAINMENT (mini bar, helicopter, limo and in-room movie) = $450.00

TOTAL: $4,176.00

Rodent Tale

Hotel Queen Leona Helmsley sued her New York law firm for $35 million because, she claims, the lawyers submitted fraudulent bills. The suit also alleges violation of the Racketeer Influenced and Corrupt Organizations Act. Included among the allegedly fraudulent items were:

- A paralegal's bill for 43 hours of time billed in a single day.
- A $124 cab fare reimbursement claimed for trips to and from the airport taken by one of her lawyers when he allegedly flew to France for a vacation.
- $148 for books, supposedly about Ms. Helmsley. Included on the list were books on wine, computers, science fiction, and a book by lawyer Alan Dershowitz entitled *Chutzpah.*
- A $238 charge for clothes from Saks Fifth Avenue.
- An $850 meal charged by partners that allegedly was concealed by the lawyers breaking it into four separate reimbursements over a two-month period.

Rodent Tale

The Fireman's Fund insurance company sued the law firm Latham & Watkins for allegedly overcharging for a number of items related to a litigation.

Among the items mentioned in Fireman's Fund complaint was an out-of-town trip by a Latham lawyer to watch another lawyer try a case. A total of ten hours at $150 an hour was charged to Fireman's Fund. The lawyer testified under oath that the trip was "part of his conscientious efforts to improve and educate himself." In papers filed with the court, Fireman's Fund called the lawyer's proclamation "the moral equivalent of a guy in a surgeon's gown, standing in a surgery room, telling the prospective heart transplant patient he is an 'experienced surgeon,' when in fact his surgical experience consisted of neutering dogs."

Finally, there was a $176.46 dinner bill from the Latham partner in charge of the case, his assistant, a jury expert, and perhaps a fourth person at a luxurious San Diego restaurant. Dinner included loin of swordfish (for two) at $41, halibut for $16.50, a special of the day at $24.75, as well as two orders of lobster scampi de la casa at $10.50 each. The total cost of the dinner came to $156.46. The tip, also charged to the client, was $20 (only thirteen percent).

The Road Trip Team

Whether it's preparing for and trying a big case or serving as counsel on a major transaction, when it comes to going out of town, The Firm always has a team of traveling lawyers and paralegals ready to go and get the job done.

Each member of The Firm's Road Trip Team has an important role to play, and teamwork is the key to effectively representing the client.

The Rainmaker.

Hasn't really practiced law in years and possesses the legal skills of a first-semester law student. Even so, he brought this client to The Firm and is going to make damn sure things are done right. His role is to castigate other team members when things go wrong and try to convince the client he knows what he's doing.

HOURLY BILLING RATE: $325.

The Real Lawyer.

The only one who knows what needs to be done and how to do it. Does ninety-five percent of the work and could have done the job all by herself. Works all night while other team members are out on the town at the client's expense. Still an associate because Rainmaker blocked her election to partnership each of the last three years.

HOURLY BILLING RATE: $250.

The Tax Attorney.

Part of any team because you never know when you'll need him (but you never do). Doesn't mind making the trip because he was sitting around doing nothing back at the office. He'll do the same here but will at least get to bill his time. Assisting Real Lawyer is out of the question because he outranks her.

HOURLY BILLING RATE: $300.

The Senior Associate.

Back at the hotel suffering the combined effects of jet lag, hangover, and disinterest. No one notices he's already three hours late.

HOURLY BILLING RATE: $240.

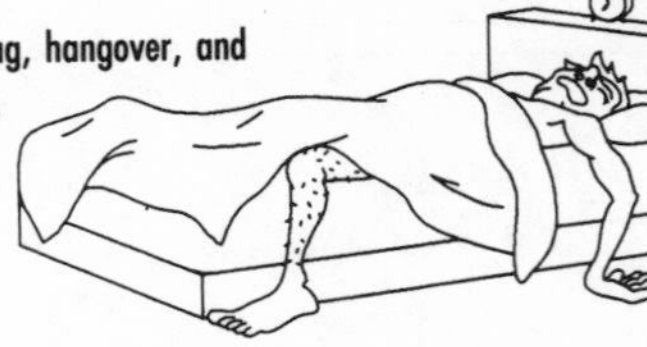

The Untried Associate.

He's just months out of law school and still waiting for his bar results. Other first-year associates are envious he made the Road Trip Team even though his only responsibility is to run back and forth to the Xerox and fax machines. At night, his job is to make sure Rainmaker doesn't get drunk and do something really stupid in front of the client.

HOURLY BILLING RATE: **$130.**

The Aging Paralegal.

Just because he didn't go to law school doesn't mean he has to do the work Untried Associate can just as easily do. Was put on the team as a favor from Rainmaker because his sister lives here and his favorite ball team also happens to be in town. He stops by for donuts and coffee in the morning but then disappears for the rest of the day.

HOURLY BILLING RATE: **$110.**

The Bankruptcy Associate.

There are no bankruptcy issues here but Rainmaker insisted she be put on the Road Trip Team after he spotted her in The Firm's library. Could help out Untried Associate but instead spends all day reading fashion magazines, talking on the phone with friends back home, eating snacks from the hotel's mini bar, and making plans for dinner with an old boyfriend who lives in town.

HOURLY BILLING RATE: **$170.**

The Hated Rival.

A very capable lawyer but Real Lawyer feels threatened by him and refuses to include him on any of the work. Spends entire trip working on other clients' files.

HOURLY BILLING RATE: **$250.**

The Left Behind Paralegal.

Was on The Road Trip Team for years until Aging Paralegal was picked for this trip. Doesn't know what he did wrong and Rainmaker hasn't returned his numerous phone calls. Last night, he ransacked Aging Paralegal's office and deleted his computer files. To get revenge he commits hara-kiri in The Firm's lobby.

ATTORNEY EGOMETER

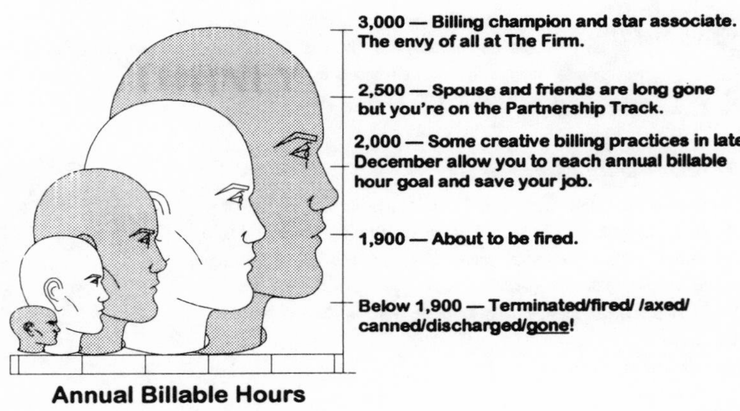

Rodent Tales

A large New York firm included in its bill to clients under the title "professional services" work done by records clerks ($70 an hour), librarians ($60 an hour), secretaries ($44 an hour), proofreaders ($35 an hour), and copy machine operators ($30 an hour).

• Another New York firm charged its client $47,890 over a three-year period for conference rooms within the law firm's office.

• A client of a Chicago firm was charged $85.01 for a thirty-one-minute fax. The amount represents $7.51 for the cost of the call and $77.50 for the firm's surcharge on faxes.

• A client of a California firm often saw an entry entitled "HVAC" on its monthly bill. The client assumed this was a computer research program but later learned that it represented charges for heating, ventilation, and air-conditioning.

• A New York law firm charged clients for pencils, pens, and file folders.

• A New York lawyer has been accused of charging clients as much as $225,000 for personal expenses, including part of the cost of his son's wedding.

Riding First Class for Fun and Profit

Lawyers love to travel not only because it gets them away from The Firm and family for a few days, but also because it is highly profitable. While lawyers charge clients at the usual hourly billing rate for every minute they are en route, additional travel expenses pave the road to a lawyer's business trip with gold. Listed below are those travel expenses most commonly incurred during lawyers' business trips and The Firm's recommendations for dealing with each one.

Hotel Mini Bar and Room Service

Recommendation: *Bill it.* All lawyers appreciate the important role hotel mini bars and room service play in the practice of law. Young lawyers are trained to make optimum use of hotel menus and in proper procedures for daily depletion of the hotel mini bar. Adding thirty percent surcharges to a $14.00 one-ounce bottle of gin and that $24.00 cheeseburger before sending the bill to the client is what makes the business trip a success.

Airplane Seat Assignment

Recommendation: *Bill for First Class.* Real lawyers don't fly coach. Besides, one needs to be comfortable billing $200 an hour for watching the in-flight movie and sipping champagne. Travel Tip: If the client is on the same flight, it's always a nice touch to have the flight attendant take a drink to him back in the coach section of the plane.

Lawyers never work while in the air because they like to charge clients their usual billable hour rate for the time it takes getting to their destination. Since the clock is running, this time is better spent relaxing. If the lawyer has any work to do in preparation for the next day's meeting, he or she will wait until arrival at the hotel so that time can be added to the day's billable hour tally.

Entertainment

Recommendation: *Bill it.* Usual items such as Broadway shows, helicopter tours of the city, and box seats at the ball game present no problem. Some clients might take issue, however, with expenses incurred for escort services and in-room porno movies. Go ahead and lump them in with laundry, haircuts, manicures, and the private masseuse. Label them "miscellaneous expenses."

Phone Calls

Recommendation: *Bill it.* Traveling can be lonely and what better time to keep in touch with old friends or try to contact lost relatives in foreign lands.

Gifts

Recommendation: *Bill it.* After working so hard and doing a great job, lawyers know that most clients won't mind if they pick up a little something for themselves. It's also nice to bring back a gift for one's secretary. If you anticipate a client objecting to this travel expense, buy something for the client. (Clients can't object to this—even if they are paying for their own gifts.)

Sleeping

Recommendation: While all lawyers have heard stories of lawyers billing for the time they spend sleeping on business trips, this is apparently only Firm fable and a gross exaggeration of how far lawyers will go. Well, okay, maybe it's not a gross exaggeration, but attorneys actually show discretion in "sleep billing" and do so only in special cases.

Some lawyers feign fear of flying and travel by Amtrak sleeper car to their destination. This way, just like on the airplane, the lawyer can charge for travel time and simultaneously get a good night's sleep billing before the big meeting in the morning. All aboard!

Rodent Tales

Although he lived in San Diego, a partner from a major firm stayed at a San Diego hotel during a six-week trial. In addition to the hotel bill, the partner charged the client for a $176 dinner, toiletries, and tobacco. The firm even charged the client for $50 stolen from a lawyer's hotel room. (It is not clear if $50 was actually stolen or a smaller amount with a surcharge added.)

A client of the firm Jeffer, Mangels claims that one of the lawyers forgot to check out of a hotel room and the client was charged for seven nights the room sat empty. The same client claimed it was asked to pay for disco admission, theater tickets, and the use of a hotel spa. Said a partner on behalf of Jeffer, Mangels: "While it's probably true that while staying away on business, use of the hotel spa was charged to the client, there seems to be nothing unusual or improper about that practice."

A Cleveland lawyer who traveled to Houston to try a case billed the client $5,000 for a week's hotel stay. When legal bill auditors reviewed the hotel bill, they found that suits, shirts, ties, and underwear at the hotel clothing store were charged to the client. The lawyer explained these expenses by saying that the trial had gone on longer than expected and he ran out of clothes.

5

Nibbling the Hand That Feeds You: King Client

Without clients, there would be no lawyers. Without lawyers, there would be far fewer clients. Fortunately, for lawyers, there are lots of clients, which leads to even more lawyers, which, in turn, leads to even more clients, and so on, and so on . . .

Most importantly, without clients, there also would be no Firm. All lawyers know this very well and therefore pay homage to King Client.

Rodent's Firmiliar Quotations

Four score and seven hours, I billed the client.

—Honest Abe Lincoln describing the bill he sent to a client for court pleadings that actually took only twenty-five hours to prepare

Rodent Tale

A California divorce lawyer was disciplined by the state bar for hiring models to flirt with married men in bars and then hand out his business card.

Those attorneys who can bring clients to The Firm reap the tremendous benefits of power and prestige. In fact, successful business developers are more valuable to The Firm today than are expert litigators and corporate lawyers. As a result, there are many lawyers who forgo the messy business of knowing the law and developing legal skills. Instead, these attorneys choose business development as a career. These are the rainmakers, who ride their clients all the way to successful careers at The Firm.

It's client beware. Lawyers are looking for you.

Doing the Law Firm Rain Dance

All play and no work make the Rainmaker a rich attorney.

Most lawyers grind through their careers spending countless hours researching obscure legal questions posed by unappreciative clients, drafting lengthy documents, and running back and forth to court. Rainmakers, on the other hand, make much more money by spending most of their time on the golf course, at The Club, and in overpriced restaurants. Having as few as two or three blue chip clients can enable an attorney to sail through his career without even touching any of the dreadful legal work that other lawyers do.

The Rainmaker's role is to reel in and then entertain clients while others do the real work. Because he spends all his time entertaining, making cold calls, and producing dog and pony shows for potential clients, the Rainmaker's legal skills dramatically deteriorate. Eventually things get so bad that when a client comes in with a problem, all the Rainmaker can say in response is: "Relax. We'll take care of it. How about the opera this weekend?"

Rainmakers are The Firm's slightly refined version of ambulance chasers and are always on the scene, business card in hand, representing themselves as legal experts on just about every conceivable area of the law. A potential client asks: "Does your firm do [anything from corporate takeovers to slip and fall work]?" The Rainmaker's reflex response is, "Of course, that's my specialty."

The Rainmakers

Vulture

The Vulture Attorney specializes in encouraging clients to sue when there's no real cause of action. Some Vultures have been known to hook up with fellow Vultures working at other firms. The two sue each other's clients back and forth until the clients end up bankrupt. The Vulture also specializes in bankruptcy law.

Parachute Attorney

The Parachute Attorney specializes in huge disasters such as explosions at chemical plants, airplane and train crashes, floods, earthquakes, fires, and other events creating an abundance of victims/clients. The Parachute Attorney strikes while the iron is hot (i.e., the bodies are still warm) by traveling to the site of the disaster, feigning sympathy for the victims and their survivors, and then hitting them with sales pitches.

THE FIRM

Internal Memorandum

TO: All Associates
FROM: The Partners
RE: Business Development

A number of associates have expressed interest in learning how to bring new clients to The Firm. The partners have therefore agreed to share some tips that many of us have found useful.

The key to developing business is joining groups and organizations that facilitate making the contacts necessary to get referrals. The more organizations you join, the better your chances of falsely befriending someone in need of legal counsel. We suggest joining each of the following:

Downtown Clubs. There's nothing better for developing business than a game of squash or pool with a director of a major corporation at an exclusive downtown club. Lying around naked in the steam room or on the masseuse's table after the game, you'll have a golden opportunity to form the bonds that lead to referrals. You'll know things are going well if you get slapped on the butt with a potential client's rolled-up towel. The Club is also a great place to start rumors about the collapse of rival firms or the imminent disbarment of the lawyer your fellow member is currently using.

Open-to-All, Egalitarian Athletic Clubs. Join one of these clubs if you want to be appointed to the Supreme Court someday and don't want to be associated with a club that has a history of discrimination. While you won't pick up the heavy hitters here, small and midsize clients can often be found. These clubs are also excellent training grounds for junior associates.

Places of Worship. Share your faith with people who will put their faith in The Firm. In the legal world, "born again" is synonymous with learning that a lawyer's spirituality can help bring in business. Don't make the mistake of limiting yourself to one religion. Try a new place of worship each month! Be a Jew on Saturday, a gentile on Sunday!

Charitable Organizations. Decide whether a cause is worthy based on who is active with the organization and how much legal work they may be able to give you.

Group Therapy. Clients are often most vulnerable to a sales pitch after baring their soul to strangers.

Family. It's always a big career boost to come from a family prominent in the business community. If you screw up on this, be sure to marry well.

Rodent Tale

After the explosion at its plant in Bhopal, India, Union Carbide had almost as many lawyers knocking on its door as it did victims.

"We were literally inundated with offers to help us with the India matter," said an in-house lawyer for Carbide. "All made carbon copies of the same pitch. They positioned themselves as experts in mass litigation, and, as a sweetener, claimed to have inside connections with the Indian government. You'd be surprised to learn how many law firms have personal relationships with the Gandhi family."

Rodent Tale

"I'm proud I'm a hustler . . . because the best lawyer in the United States is the lawyer [who] has the best client.

"[What I tell young lawyers is] go out and meet people. Don't go home at five-thirty to your wife and kids every night, okay? I mean, that's nice—[but] go out and have dinner, go to parties. The only way to get business is to make your presence felt. You've got to go and hustle."

—Dan Webb, litigation partner at the Chicago firm Winston & Strawn

ATTORNEY EGOMETER

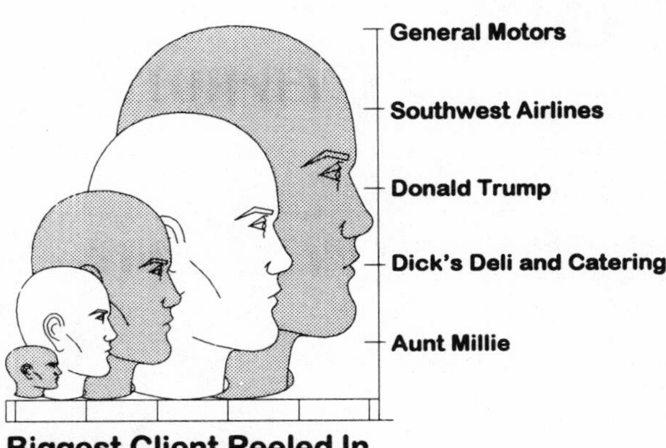

▪ *Fishing for Clients* ▪

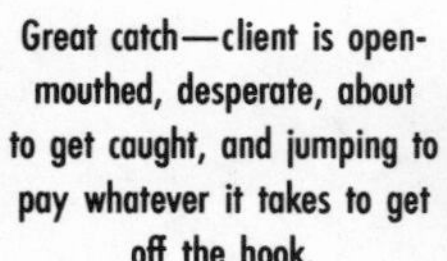

Great catch—client is open-mouthed, desperate, about to get caught, and jumping to pay whatever it takes to get off the hook.

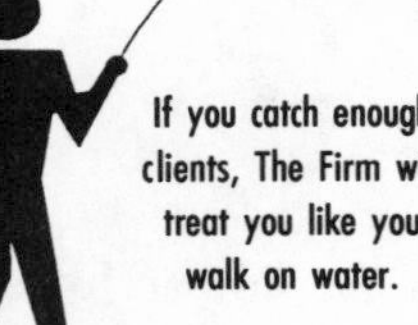

If you catch enough clients, The Firm will treat you like you walk on water.

Watch Out!!! It's another lawyer looking for some-one to take his malpractice case!

At The Firm, you eat what you catch. This client is tasty enough to take your career upstream.

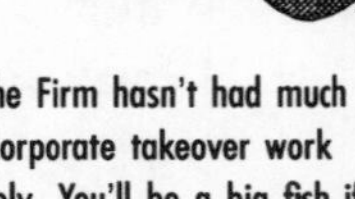

The Firm hasn't had much corporate takeover work lately. You'll be a big fish if you reel this one in.

Bait.

Something's fishy. You've spent a lot of time and money trying to lure this one in, but no bites.

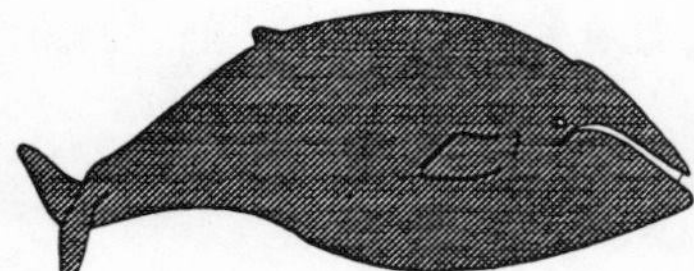

Great catch! This is what client stories are made of—huge with lots of blubber. Bill freely!

"You should have seen the one that got caught by the FDIC."

You have bigger clients to fry. Throw this one back in.

This one can't pay its bill and could be deadly to your career.

Be careful. This client seems like the catch of the day but is known to sting lawyers by suing for malpractice.

Beware of the competition smelling blood in these client-infested waters.

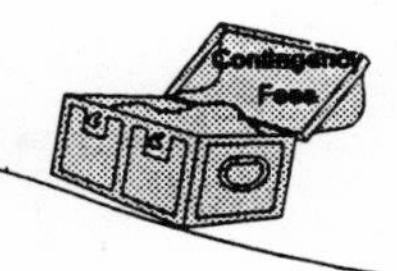

The Client Meeting

Clients often are curious about two things when The Firm calls a meeting on their nickel: first, why so many lawyers are needed, and second, what role each one plays in getting the job done. To help answer these questions, we drop in on a typical lawyers' meeting at The Firm and into the mind of each lawyer while the client explains his legal problems.

Law Firm Lingo

The Lawyer Letter: A Translation

Rata & Raton
900 Avenue of the Attorneys
Boca Raton, Florida 33431
(407) 555-2300

Snoop Doggy Dog
Nadine Sutherland
Da Brat
C. L. Smooth
Brian McNight
Queen Latifah

1

Salt N Pepa
Bossman Blakjak
Dr. Dre
Ice Cube Ill Al Skratch
Big Daddy Kane
Mic Geronimo
Da Youngsta's
Wu-Tang Clan
Smif N. Wessun
Fu Schnickens

August 14, 1995[2]

Our file number: 0150-99990-1[3]

Via Fax, Federal Express, UPS and U.S. Mail[4]

Ms. Clara Client
Rodent Publications
International Executive Headquarters
2531 Sawtelle Boulevard #30
Los Angeles, California 90064

RE: The American Bar Association v. The Rodent[5]

Dear Ms. Client:

This letter is in response to our telephonic communication[6] pertaining to the above-referenced matter (the "Litigation").[7] In furtherance thereto,[8] enclosed please find copies of Section 1002.3(c) of the Corporations Code.

In connection thereto, we are also enclosing a memorandum we prepared on your behalf concerning the tax advantages of reincorporating under the laws of the Cayman Islands.[9] Also enclosed is our compare/contrast analysis of traditional English common law and continental European civil law with which we thought you should be familiar.[10]

Please do not hesitate to contact me should you have any questions concerning the Litigation or any other matter.

Very truly yours,

Emily Bestler
for The Firm[11]

cc: Jeni D. Catch, Esq.[12] (w/enclosures)[13]
Bryant H. Byrnes, Esq. (w/enclosures)
Linda B. Ross, Esq. (w/enclosures)
Stuart Thompson, Esq. (w/enclosures)[14]

1. The Great Divide.
2. Letters are often predated to make up for missed deadlines.
3. Every document identified for easy billing. (See number 13 below.)
4. Quadruple surcharge!
5. In case the client can't figure out what the hell the lawyer is talking about.
6. What other people call a "phone call."
7. Lawyers love these definitions inside parentheses and brackets.
8. Sprinkling in a little Lawyerese "here and there"—Hereto, thereto. Hereas, thereas. Hereby, thereby. Heretofore, theretofore. Hereunder, thereunder. Herein, therein.
9. Good lawyers always do more than what is expected of them. This leads to attorney fees that are more than what is expected.
10. This might be too much.
11. In case lawyer is sued for malpractice, she can claim to be acting on behalf of The Firm and hopefully escape personal liability.
12. Lawyers can't call themselves doctors so they use this "Esq." thing to separate themselves from other members of society.
13. At fifty cents a page, make as many copies as possible. Some of these lawyers aren't even on the case but will still bill the client for the time it takes to read this letter and the enclosures (even if they don't actually read them).
14. Always wait a day or two before sending copies to partners so that typographical errors or bad advice can be corrected and the partners won't see the slop sent out to the client.

6

Pest Control: Family, Friends, and Interoffice Interaction

Business and Pleasure

During their years as associates, lawyers at The Firm are forced to work so hard and are so preoccupied with keeping on the Partnership Track that they don't have time

Rodent's Firmiliar Quotations

If you can't be with the one you love, love the one you work with.

—Partner Stephen Stills of Crosby, Stills & Nash, attorneys at law

for a social life *outside the office.* Anyone or anything not directly advancing their careers becomes an inconvenience.

Most of the friends the lawyer had upon entering law school are long gone by the time she starts at The Firm. They grew tired of being neglected and bored by oft-repeated stories concerning the dull details of law school and legal work.

Fortunately, lawyers don't have to venture far for social activities as The Firm offers plenty of outlets for nonbillable time. Most lawyers replace their lifetime friends with potential clients. When planning social events, they always include someone in a position to refer business to The Firm.

Anyone who once played an important part in the lawyer's life is soon forgotten as The Firm becomes the lawyer's family, best friend, lover, and God.

Rodent Tale

When Steven Kumble's aunt asked him to represent her on a $1,800 matter, he referred her to one of his partners. In so doing, Attorney Kumble instructed the other lawyer: "You tell her that the minimum retainer is $2,500."

"But, Steve," the partner responded, "she's your aunt. We can't charge her $2,500 for an $1,800 problem."

"Aunt, schmant," said Attorney Kumble. "If she can't pay her retainer, she can go elsewhere."

THE FIRM
Internal Memorandum

TO: All New Associates
FROM: The Office Manager
RE: Love at The Firm

Upon beginning work at The Firm, all associates pledge not to become romantically involved with anyone from the office. At first, you will find it easy to keep the promise because colleagues will seem annoying and repulsive. After you have been here for a few months and begin losing contact with the outside, however, others at The Firm will continue to seem just as annoying and repulsive, but somehow now suitable and desirable. Interoffice interaction is inevitable.

Let the interoffice romance begin! Lawyers must, however, follow certain guidelines to get the most out of their office romance.

1. Deny all rumors of involvement with someone at The Firm. While you may think your office love affair is a big secret, everyone else will know what's going on and you may be confronted about the liaison. The key to successful interoffice romance is plausible deniability. One effective response is: "You have misinformation, he/she is sleeping with [name of your Hated Rival(s)]."

2. Don't pursue the Senior Partner's secretary. Why do you think this person is the Senior Partner's secretary?

3. Schedule romantic encounters around certain events, e.g., waiting for documents to be copied or typed, during conference calls, etc. This way, you can bill clients and date at the same time.

4. Don't date anyone ranking above you at The Firm. Partners should date associates, paralegals, secretaries, etc. Senior associates should date junior associates, paralegals, and so on. This way, when things go sour, you can use your senior position to have your former law firm lover fired.

5. Send your Dear John/Jane letter via E-mail for fastest action. This avoids leaving a paper trail that might be used by a former special law firm friend trying to prove the relationship to a jury. If you

anticipate being the plaintiff in such a suit, save all correspondence, receipts for hotel and meal reimbursements the two of you run up on a client's expense account, etc. These items can be very helpful as evidence.

6. Keep your résumé current.

Rodent Tale

On the subject of law firm romance, the magazine *California Lawyer* reported the following comments from participants:

- "You're with these people all the time, it's a them-versus-us mentality. Pretty soon, your hormones are acting up. The camaraderie, especially when you're winning, is exhilarating. The life you may have at home—the boring tax accountant husband, the nagging wife and three kids—isn't nearly as exciting as the life you have with the person in your office."
- "Lawyers are attracted to each other because we repel everybody else."
- "Our arguments are like arguments before the Supreme Court."
- "My wife is one of the perks from that year in the public defender's office. I cite her as a side benefit of doing pro bono work."
- "It's best not to tell anyone."
- "One of the benefits of interoffice romance is that you are often both anxious about the same thing."

Rodent Tales

Dream Dresser is a Washington, D.C., "department store for fantasy fashions and accessories." In response to an advertisement it placed in *Legal Times,* the city's legal newspaper, the store received "tons of faxes" on law firm letterheads requesting copies of the store's catalogue. Said the store owner, "Lawyers are not known [as sexy]. Neither are Republicans. But they both are my best customers."

A shop called Stormy Leather, which specializes in latex and fetish wear for women, placed an advertisement in *The Recorder,* a San Francisco legal newspaper. The store manager said she placed the ad because "All the major surveys show that of all the people into S&M and [the] leather scene, the two most common groups are psychotherapists and lawyers."

Home: Office Away from Office

After a couple of years of practicing law, associates begin to believe they actually are worth $200 an hour. When a lawyer realizes that he can't get away with charging family members his usual rate, time spent away from the office starts to seem like a big waste. A movie with the spouse, for

Rodent Tale

In its June 1991 issue, *Ebony* magazine named attorney Derrick Walker as one of the best bachelor catches of the year. The magazine described him as a thirty-one-year-old bachelor who is "a horseback riding enthusiast and prefers a warm, athletic woman."

The Drug Enforcement Administration also saw Attorney Walker as a great catch. It seems he was under investigation for using his lawyer connections to broker cocaine deals.

Attorney Walker is no longer practicing law because he was sentenced to fifteen and a half years in prison on federal cocaine charges. The term was enhanced because the bachelor abused his position of trust as a lawyer. He is also no longer a bachelor as he was married in a ceremony at the U.S. Marshal's office, performed by the judge who sentenced him.

example, is a loss of $400 in billable time. Dinner is another $300. A weekend is thousands of dollars worth of time that could have been devoted to a client.

Because divorce and child abandonment reflect poorly on the lawyer, other steps are taken to put the family in its place and make the best of an unfortunate situation.

The Lawyer's Family

After working two or three jobs for tuition money and writing most of the lawyer's research papers throughout college and law school, the lawyer's spouse plays a far more limited role now that the lawyer is at The Firm.

If the spouse is attractive, she can be used to score points at The Firm's social gatherings. The associate should instruct the spouse to entertain partners. If the spouse is not so attractive, the lawyer should call ***Surrogate Lawyers*** (see advertisement on page 193).

Spouses can also be used to take the blame for late projects and breaking off interoffice romances. Children can be trained to pass out mom or dad's business card and do legal research (billed to the client at the lawyer's usual hourly rate).

The Lawyer's Friends

The only friends worth having are those who can advance the attorney's career.

After the bar exam, friends of the lawyer's youth begin to drop off, having grown tired of repeated cancellations and attempts to solicit business by their former buddy. To fill the void, the lawyer finds new friends from major corporations who are in a position to refer legal work to The Firm.

As the lawyer becomes more senior, those ranking below her at The Firm will pretend to be her friend for their own selfish purposes. Even though they ridicule the lonesome attorney behind her back, these false friends offer the companionship and warmth lacking in the lawyer's life.

A partner's only real friends are other partners until, of course, the partner becomes an economic drain on The Firm. When this occurs, The Partner is forced out of The Firm and left friendless.

The Associate's "Week at a Glance"

Monday. Work, sleep. Brag about working all weekend long.

Tuesday. Work, sleep. Free donuts! (Highlight of the week.)

Wednesday. Work, no sleep. Hump day! Buy something expensive for the wife to make up for not seeing her this weekend.

Thursday. Work, sleep at office (but tell everyone it was another all-nighter).

Friday. Work, sleep. TGIF! Before sending messenger out to the house, have secretary draft letter to wife to go with expensive gift.

Saturday. Work, casual clothes day. "If you don't come in Saturday, don't bother coming in Sunday!"

Sunday. Work, call kids, sleep. Only 312 more weeks until partnership!

Rodent Tale

For purposes of expense reimbursement, Gary Fairchild, a former partner at Chicago's Winston & Strawn, was reportedly in the habit of presenting his firm with photocopies of personal checks made out to charities, hotels, and other companies. After doing so, he supposedly tore up the checks and pocketed the reimbursements. Attorney Fairchild also was accused of submitting receipts for personal entertainment and at least one family vacation and reporting them as business expenses.

Gary Fairchild is also reported to have referred a piece of business from Winston & Strawn to his wife, Maureen, at that time a partner at Chapman and Cutler, Chicago's seventh-largest firm. Although the case sent to Mrs. Fairchild was a simple collection matter, Maureen Fairchild billed her husband's firm almost $60,000 over the next two and a half years. Even after the case was dismissed, bills for as much as ten hours a day were reportedly submitted to Winston & Strawn for the matter that no longer existed. The total amount billed to Winston & Strawn, which eventually reached close to a quarter of a million dollars, was all approved by Gary Fairchild.

The scheme was uncovered when Mrs. Fairchild's then-partner at Chapman and Cutler, James Spiotto, accused her of overbilling. The two partners had evidently enjoyed a long relationship as Hated Rivals. Soon after Mr. Spiotto accused Mrs. Fairchild, an anonymous source sent Mr. Spiotto's billing records to a *Wall Street Journal* reporter who had written a story about the Fairchilds' dubious arrangement.

According to these billing records, Mr. Spiotto charged clients for 6,022 hours of work in 1993. That works out to sixteen and a half hours a day, every day of the year. In the preceding three years, Mr. Spiotto had billed clients at a clip of 5,000 hours a year.

Weekending at The Firm

Because lawyers at The Firm are grossly overpaid, The Firm has to compensate by hiring too few associates to do the work. In other words, instead of hiring ten associates to work normal hours for reasonable salaries, The Firm hires six or seven associates, pays them excessive salaries, and expects them to do the work of ten.

These hardworking lawyers very much look forward to the weekend, during which they can recover from their labors and prepare for the next week. The weekend also holds the following advantages for associates:

- Less traffic on the roads and it's easy to get a seat on public transit.
- The office is always open and a cheap place to take the family. Kids can run documents down to the Word Processing Department to be typed.

- Saturdays and Sundays are a great time to steal office supplies, rummage through other lawyers' desks, and crack a Hated Rival's computer and voice mail codes.
- Weekends facilitate using Hated Rival's office to send nasty messages to other lawyers, the Office Manager, and the Senior Executive Secretary from his phone extension and E-mail.

Rodent Tale

Skadden, Arps's Joe Flom told his partner Les Arps of his plans to get married. Arps responded by saying he had a diamond ring for Flom's fiancée. Evidently he had given the ring to someone he planned to marry but then changed his mind and took it back.

After Arps retrieved the ring from the firm vault and gave it to Flom, Flom asked his future wife Claire to stop by the firm. Flom slipped the ring on Claire's finger, and then he and Arps went back to work.

When a friend of hers complimented Claire Flom on the ring, she replied, "Les Arps gave it to me."

Legal Holidays

Every lawyer who has ever worked at The Firm carries a special holiday memory. Perhaps it is sleeping on a cold airport floor after working late and missing the last Christmas Eve flight out of town. An associate may recall the joy of trying to deliver a document to a partner's vacation home, having the car skid off the road, and spending days in a snowbank fighting off frostbite. For others, it is the thought of the family gathered around the fireplace or opening presents when the lawyer calls from the office to say it will be another seven or eight more hours before she can get home for the holiday.

It is these memories that teach attorneys the true meaning of the legal holidays.

T H E   F I R M

Internal Memorandum

TO: All Associates

FROM: The Partners

RE: Christmas at The Firm

DATE: December 24

The Firm will be "officially" closed tomorrow for Christmas. For those associates who will be working (and we expect that will be most of you), we'd like to make the holiday a joyous occasion and thus provide a few tips for assuring you get the most out of Christmas at The Firm.

1. Buy yourself a present on the way to the office (7-Eleven is open twenty-four hours) and open it while waiting for documents to come out of the Word Processing Department.

2. Bring a cassette tape of Christmas carols and listen to them on your dictaphone.

3. In lieu of going to church with loved ones, gather for services in the Senior Partner's office.

4. Order Christmas dinner from Domino's. Unlike The Firm, Domino's is understaffed on holidays and you may get two dollars off when they fail to deliver within thirty minutes.

5. Feel fortunate that your post-Christmas depression has kicked in early and this year you might feel like celebrating on New Year's Eve.

6. Come in dressed as your favorite biblical character.

7. Use the fire extinguisher to make your office part of a white Christmas.

Merry Christmas and Happy New Fiscal Year!

T H E   F I R M

Holiday Party Notice

MARK THE DATE!   HOLIDAY PARTIES SET

ATTORNEYS' PARTY

The annual holiday attorneys' party is set for December 19 and will be held in the Grand Ballroom of the fabulous new Four Seasons Hotel. Entertainment will be provided by Ray Charles, Jay Leno, and a surprise guest you just won't believe!

The Firm has reserved a block of hotel suites and a fleet of limousines for the occasion. Please let us know how many you will need for the evening and how many guests you expect to attend. Sorry, only three suites per attorney.

STAFF PARTY

This year's staff party will be a pot luck in the thirty-seventh-floor lunchroom on December 24 from 6:30 P.M. until 9:00 P.M. The Office Manager will use the occasion to explain the cutbacks in The Firm's benefits package that take effect on January 1. The cost is fifteen dollars. Attendance is mandatory.

▪ *The Firm's Party Survival Guide* ▪

For the associate, nothing at The Firm is easy—not even the parties. Throughout the year, The Firm hosts various social events to mark special occasions such as a major holiday, the election of an attorney to partnership, the winning of a big sexual harassment lawsuit brought against one of the partners, or the termination of a batch of associates.

With partners in attendance, associates know their every move is being watched and evaluated. In essence, The Firm's social gatherings are always extremely stressful experiences for associates. Among the risks you run by attending a Firm social function are:

- Some staff member with a previously unexpressed passion for you will cling to your side throughout the evening. Everyone will be watching with great amusement as you try to deal with this delicate situation.

- The Lecherous Partner may ask you to dance to one of those long slow songs. You're an associate and in no position to say no and, again, the eyes of The Firm (and the partner's hands) will be on you.

- You might get drunk and tell some partners what you really think of them.
- Your secretary may use the occasion to tell you in front of the entire Firm exactly what she thinks of you.
- Even if you're perfectly behaved, your Hated Rival may start vicious rumors about things you did at the party and you'll go down in Firm history for the nonevent. Remember, your career can just as easily be ruined by something you didn't do as for something you did.

Basically, The Firm's parties are just too risky for associates and the best thing to do is stay away. If, however, an associate chooses to attend the party, there are a number of things that can be done to make the most out of the occasion. Some maneuvers that have worked well over the years include:

- Retaining a child actor to interrupt the party by claiming to be your Hated Rival's illegitimate, abandoned child.
- Remembering that where you sit determines where you stand. Arrive at the party an hour beforehand to rearrange the seat assignments. Seat yourself with The Firm's Power Partners. Seat your Hated Rival with Puny Partners and the associates who everyone knows are about to be forced out of The Firm. Fill out the rest of the table with the Mail Guy, the unpopular office manager (redundant), the Runt Associate, and The Firm's controller, who is currently under investigation for embezzlement. This will create the impression of a losers' table and seriously injure your Hated Rival.
- Starting vicious rumors about your Hated Rival and something she did at the party after everyone has had a

few drinks. Better yet, select two Hated Rivals and make up a story about something they did together.

- Making sure that the person you are seen leaving the party with is in good standing because, even if you just happen to walk out at the same time, you will be linked to that person sexually forever in the annals of The Firm's history. (Please try to avoid crowding when Power Partners leave the room.)

Enjoy the party!

ATTORNEY EGOMETER

The Law Firm Party

Lawyer Leagues

For some reason, actually for no reason at all, lawyers take their sports very seriously. They form lawyer leagues and compete against other law firms. They also cheat against other firms—mostly because The Firm's lawyers hate to lose, even when there's nothing at stake. Most Lawyer League games quickly deteriorate into shoving matches, long arguments, and threats. Individual lawyers, law firms, referees, and the league itself are often sued by losing teams—all in the name of sportsmanship.

▪ *The Law Firm's Starting Lineup* ▪

PLAYER: Hard-charging associate
SKILLS: Talking trash and starting fights. Leads the Lawyer League in technical fouls.

ROLE ON TEAM: As team captain, he makes sure at least five people break away from their work at The Firm and show up for each game.

FAVORITE PROFESSIONAL: Chris Webber.

PLAYER: Partner

SKILLS: Overweight, slow, bad knees, specializes in calling time-outs.

ROLE ON TEAM: Because he is a partner, everyone passes him the ball and encourages him to shoot. Back at the office the next day, teammates tell everyone how he carried the team with that one shot (out of thirty attempts) he made.

FAVORITE PROFESSIONAL: Bob Cousey.

PLAYER: Mail Guy

SKILLS: Former high school All-American, he's a ringer in this league.

ROLE ON TEAM: The subject of a class action lawsuit brought by losing teams who suspect he isn't a lawyer and thus is ineligible to play in the Lawyer League.

FAVORITE PROFESSIONAL: Karl "The Mailman" Malone.

PLAYER: Female Litigator

SKILLS: Clearly the best lawyer on the team. Her forte is offensive rebounding, the low-bridge foul, and the ally-oop pass to the Mail Guy for the slam dunk.

ROLE ON TEAM: To show The Firm's sexist male lawyers that women are just as good as men.

FAVORITE PROFESSIONAL: Shaquille O'Neal.

PLAYER: Tax Attorney

SKILLS: Specialist in international tax shelters.

ROLE ON TEAM: To be the fifth person to show up for the game and thus keep the team from losing by default.

FAVORITE PROFESSIONAL: Kristi Yamaguchi.

THE FIRM

Notice

Sign up Now for Lawyer Games!

It's time once again for the annual Lawyer Games to be held downtown next month. The Firm encourages all its "athletes" (i.e., no one from the Tax Department) to sign up and help us compete against the city's other law firms. This year's Lawyers Games will include the following competitions:

1. Synchronized Billing
2. State Bar Ethics Committee Sprint
3. Billathon
4. Paralegal Toss
5. Litigation Brief Filing Relay
6. Uneven Billing Competition
7. Roman-Greco Corner Office Vacancy Wrestle
8. Free-Style Billing
9. High Hourly Billing Rate Jump
10. Partner Put
11. Client Chase
12. Cross Country Run Up the Client's Expense Account

7

The Big Cheese: Partnerhood

Election to partnership is The Firm's Holy Grail and the payoff for all a lawyer's hard work, preparation, and suffering—going all the way back to her days as a Baby Barrister. Achieving partnership status is also a symbol that the lawyer has successfully played the Partnership Game and either: (a) demonstrated a mastery of the law or, as is more likely the case, (b) fooled enough people into thinking she is a

Rodent's Firmiliar Quotations

We have nothing to fear but declining revenues, being hit with a big malpractice suit, having our insurance canceled, insolent staff, disloyal clients, losing our lease, disbarment, defections to other firms, the Senior Executive Secretary, and ourselves.

—The Managing Partner's opening statement at The Firm's annual partnership meeting

great lawyer or enough clients into retaining The Firm so that the partners can't afford to fire her.

Life above the line is supposed to be much easier than associate life. Partners get to sit back, boss everyone else around, assign projects on Friday afternoon, count The Firm's money, fire subordinates on a whim, and become rich on the backs of the hard labor of others. The best thing about the promotion, however, is no longer being an associate and getting to reap the rewards waiting in the Promised Land of Partnership.

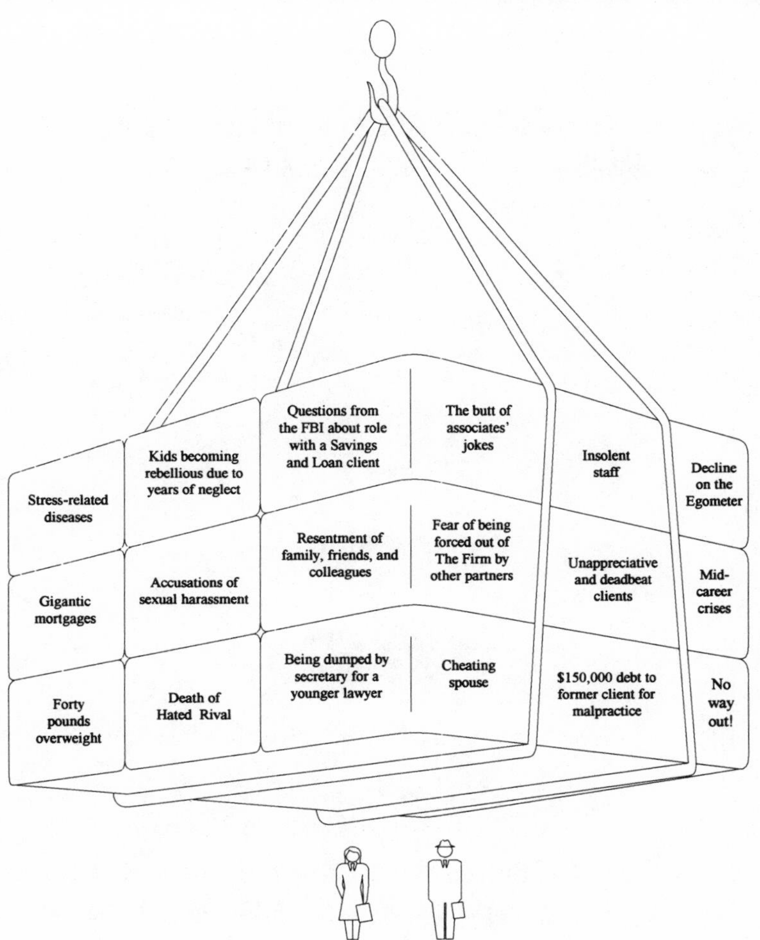

The Promised Land of Partnership Pressures

After a decade or so of hard work and sacrifice at The Firm, fortunate attorneys reach the pinnacle of lawyerdom—the Promised Land of Partnership. Everything lawyers ever wanted and hoped for is finally theirs!

ATTORNEY EGOMETER

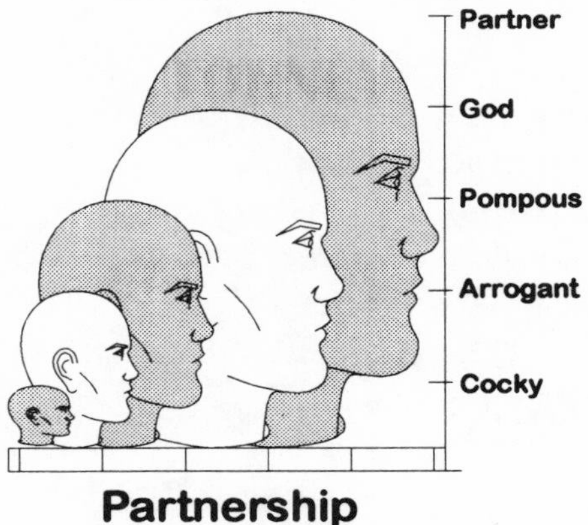

Rodent Tale

"Part of this nightmare is that I'll end up like the senior partner I'm working for now. Everyone agrees he is a great lawyer—one of the best in the firm—but, Jesus, what a drone! He's now on a nine-day vacation, his first in years. He's not a young man, and he's in this firm from eight A.M. until ten P.M. Then he takes the train home, sleeps, and comes right back, time after time after time. He will wake up someday—soon!—and see only a wall of volumes of his cases. Is that it?"

—an associate from a prestigious Manhattan law firm

Playing the Partner's Role

After years of working at The Firm, most associates making the transition to partner have a good idea of how they are expected to behave in the Promised Land. This makes the transition an easy and natural process. Nevertheless, recently elected partners are reminded to follow certain basic behavioral guidelines.

Reprinted below are excerpts from "How to Play the Partner's Role," a manual The Firm distributes at the new partners' orientation program.

- Wait until 5:00 P.M. on Friday to assign projects to associates. Demand to have work completed and on your desk by Monday morning.

- When assigning the project, give the associate complex and convoluted instructions. If the associate asks a question or indicates any lack of understanding, roll your eyes, sigh, and ask with a tone of annoyance in your voice, "Where did you go to law school?"

- Calculate how many hours you think it will take the associate to complete the work. Tell the associate not to spend more than one third of that time on the assignment.

- While the associate is working on the assignment, have your secretary call him every hour to ask if it's completed yet.

- After the associate works all weekend on the assignment, take two or three weeks to review the draft. Ignore all substantive aspects of the work but be sure to severely criticize the associate for any grammatical or typographical errors.

- Have the associate come to your office to discuss the project. While he is waiting to talk to you, make personal phone calls, finish reading a few documents on your desk, and dictate a letter to your valet. Every five or ten minutes, tell the associate, "This will only take a second, just stay where you are."
- If the work product is impressive, have the associate turn it into an article and send it out for publication under your name. If the client complains, the state bar comes knocking, or The Firm is hit with a big malpractice suit, give the associate full credit for the assignment.
- When the client doesn't pay the bill, apply the amount of the retainer to your account and write down the associate's time without explaining why.

Partner Power

With so many asses at The Firm, it's difficult for the associate to know which ones to kiss. This determination is crucial because an associate's career can hinge on the fortunes of the partner she decides to latch onto. By carefully selecting the right partner, any associate—no matter how unqualified and incompetent—can assure her success. Here's what to look for in a partner.

Power Partner

1. Takes three days to return phone calls from clients and a week for calls from other lawyers. Has secretary return calls from spouse.
2. Never attends The Firm's social functions. Few associates have ever actually seen him.
3. Hasn't really practiced law in years.
4. Has diplomas from Ivy League universities on office wall, but these schools have no record of the Power Partner ever attending.
5. Has been disbarred in four states.
6. Has no idea who you are (and doesn't care).

Puny Partner

1. Recently had to sell his home to one of The Firm's paralegals due to his reduced partnership draw.
2. Knows how to operate the copying and fax machines. Answers his own telephone because he doesn't want to inconvenience his secretary.
3. Stable family life. Has never had sex in the office.
4. Stops by associates' offices just to say "hi" and is usually described as "a really nice guy."
5. Turns down cases and clients that present conflicts of interest or pose ethical and moral problems for him.
6. Power Partner knows who he is but pretends not to.

Rodent Tale

Thomas Dewey was the former New York governor who, according to press accounts, defeated Harry S. Truman for president in 1948. He was also a founder of the law firm Dewey, Ballantine, Bushby, Palmer & Wood.

One Saturday, Attorney Dewey called the office in an effort to find an associate to do some work for him. After getting a young associate on the phone, Mr. Dewey explained what he needed and then emphasized that it had to be done immediately. The associate responded that he couldn't possibly take on more work because he already expected to be at the office all weekend completing a project that was due on Monday.

Attorney Dewey, not believing what he was hearing from the associate, asked, "Do you know who this is?" When the associate replied that he did not, he was told, "This is Thomas Dewey." After a short pause, the associate asked, "Do you know who *this* is?" When Mr. Dewey said that he didn't, the associate hung up the phone.

Rodent Tale

A woman was on an airplane reading a law book when the man next to her asked if she was a lawyer. The woman responded that she practiced law at the Baton Rouge, Louisiana, office of the firm Kutak Rock.

The man told the woman he thought that was quite a coincidence because he was Harold Rock, one of the men the firm was named after. The woman didn't believe him because, as she told Mr. Rock, he was dead. Attorney Rock had to take out his American Bar Association identification card and have his wife verify his identity.

Firm Personality Profile:
▪ *The Lecherous Partner* ▪

Personal Life: Has serious mid-life crisis. Married to a madwoman.

Favorite Pastimes: Chatting with new associates, paralegals, and secretaries whose standing at The Firm precludes them from telling him to get lost. Spends most weekends at The Firm even when he doesn't have any work to do.

Career Highlight: Selected to play Santa Claus at The Firm's holiday party. Paralegal Party Girl sits on his lap and tells him what she really wants for Christmas.

Professional Reputation: He's the man to see if you are a client in litigation that could ruin you (and he happens to be sleeping with the judge hearing the case).

Future at The Firm: Put in charge of recruiting summer associates.

Firm Personality Profile: The Kind, Honest, Caring, and ▪ Generous Partner ▪

Personal Life: Happily married. Devoted to husband and kids. She knows what's important in life and work always comes second.

Favorite Pastimes: Making sure the people who work for her are happy. Volunteering her time for community projects and doing pro bono work for worthy causes.

Career Highlight: Hiring disadvantaged youth for part-time positions and developing a scholarship fund to finance their education. Donates half her salary to charity.

Professional Reputation: Highly respected for her integrity and professional skills. Honest and considerate of clients and colleagues. A role model for many of the young people who work with her.

Future at The Firm: Whoops! This one isn't even a lawyer. She's a partner at the accounting firm upstairs who got off the elevator at the wrong floor.

The Nine Stages of a Mid-Career Crisis

1. Disenchantment

Although still in love with The Firm, Lawyer feels tied down and longs to recapture the excitement he felt as a junior associate. New firms start to look attractive and Lawyer wonders what it would be like to be a sole practitioner again.

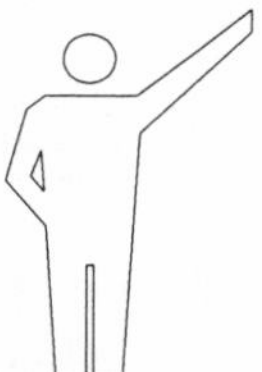

2. Wandering Eye

Lawyer becomes increasingly distracted. On the one hand, he is devoted to The Firm and grateful for all it has done for him. On the other hand, another firm would sure be a thrill. The Firm trusts Lawyer and suspects nothing.

3. Flirtation

Lawyer and the Other Firm meet at the state bar convention. They have lunch together and, a week later, Lawyer goes to Other Firm's office for dinner. Other Firm is clearly interested but Lawyer feels guilty flirting with another and fears risking everything he has worked for.

4. Consummation

Other Firm asks Lawyer to go away for the weekend. Lawyer uses the excuse of having to leave town on business for a few days and goes to Other Firm's annual retreat. When the Other Firm makes advances, the lure is too great and Lawyer is seduced.

5. Guilt and Confusion

Feeling guilty about being unfaithful to The Firm and still unsure about whether to go with Other Firm, Lawyer is confused and hesitant. Other Firm pressures Lawyer to make choice. Flattered by the attention and aroused by Other Firm, he decides to leave The Firm.

6. Preparation for Leaving

Fearful of how The Firm will react, Lawyer secretly prepares for defection. He steals files, raids The Firm's bank account, and calls clients seeking assurances they will stay with him when he goes to Other Firm. Behind closed doors, Lawyer breaks the news to shocked associates and asks them to come along. Lawyer warns this could lead to a court battle with The Firm.

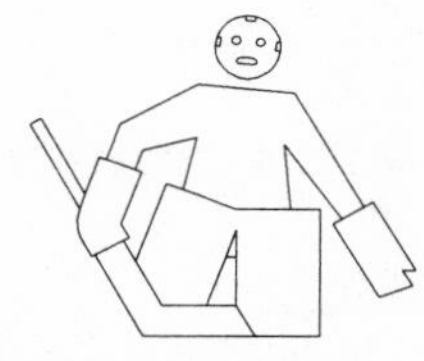

7. Found Out

The Firm discovers a note from Other Firm on Lawyer's desk and becomes hysterical. In disbelief, The Firm asks: "How could you do this? Haven't we been good to you? What about the associates?" Shock turns to anger and The Firm vows to take Lawyer for everything he's worth. The Firm calls clients seeking their support in the breakup.

8. Fade of Affection

After a few months, infatuation with Other Firm wears off. Other Firm seemed so nice during the courtship but the partners there are even meaner than those at The Firm. Lawyer misses The Firm and the old way of life he had before so foolishly leaving.

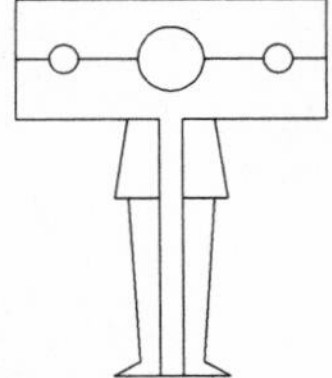

9. Forgiveness/Punishment

Lawyer breaks off relationship with Other Firm and begs The Firm to take him back. The Firm, after making Lawyer squirm for a couple of months and make promises he will never be able to keep, takes Lawyer back.

The Last Chapter: Extermination—Termination, Of Counsel, Death, and Afterlife

Rodent's Firmiliar Quotations

On the whole, I'd rather be in Philadelphia.

—Epitaph for a bar-flunker

While billing from the grave can prove difficult, some lawyers still manage to make money after their demise. If, for example, The Firm is named after a dead lawyer or if clients of the deceased continue to retain The Firm, the dead lawyer is still able to turn a profit. Thus, for lawyers, death really isn't so bad.

More devastating than actual physical death are the many deaths an attorney's ego suffers over the course of a career. And of those many deaths, the absolute worst is when The Firm decides it's time to rid itself of the lawyer.

The Firm has several methods of execution. First, there is the termination of employment that almost all lawyers periodically experience during their careers. Later on, there's The Firm-created category known as "Of Counsel." The Of Counsel designation is used by partners to dump lawyers who have outlived their usefulness. Finally, there is physical death, the most exhilarating way to leave The Firm. Although now dead, it is here in the attorney afterlife that the lawyer generates more activity at The Firm than he has in years.

Termination

At least once or twice during the course of a legal career, an associate gets knocked off the Partnership Track and his ass is fired. At The Firm, unlike most other workplaces where employees are terminated for substandard performance or a downturn in business, associates are usually let go for no good reason at all. Typically, associates can expect to be fired when:

1. *They become capable lawyers.* Competence doesn't pay at The Firm. In addition to fearing that associates will steal their clients, partners generally have poor and out-of-date legal skills. They certainly don't want to be shown up by some young buck with an encyclopedic knowledge of the law. When a client starts complimenting an associate or specifically asking that he handle the work, it's a good sign said associate is about to be terminated.

2. *The Firm's structure requires it.* Around town, a firm's reputation is generally gauged by its associate attrition rate. Common wisdom has it that a firm that makes too many of its associates partners must have very low standards. Therefore, some associates are sacrificed for the sake of protecting The Firm's reputation.

3. *Law firm tradition demands it.* Most partners were fired once or twice for no reason when they were associates and they think it only fair that others suffer the same humiliating experience. Exercising the power to terminate an associate's career is also an excellent way for partners to maintain their position on the Egometer.

4. *The Hated Rival wins.*

Rodent Tale

Although an associate had been told privately that she was being terminated due to a downturn in her firm's business, the firm refused to admit this publicly. The associate was thus left in the difficult position of disclaiming she was fired for reasons of poor performance when trying to find a new job. When she brought this to the attention of a partner, the response was "Listen . . . they would rather you feel miserable than anybody think we're on shaky ground financially."

THE FIRM

Internal Memorandum

TO: All Associates
FROM: The Recruiting Committee
RE: Your Termination

There simply isn't enough time in the day to inform associates personally when they have been canned. We therefore recommend that all associates pay close attention to indicators in and around the office that it's time to relocate to a position of alternative professional responsibility outside The Firm.

Specifically, because everyone else in the office will know about your termination before you do, look for these telltale signs that it's time to hit the road and save us the chore of having to break the tragic news:

1. Partners who once warmly greeted you suddenly fail to acknowledge your existence.
2. Partners who have never previously acknowledged your existence now warmly greet you.
3. Paralegals and junior associates stop pretending to like you.
4. The Mail Guy snickers whenever he sees you.
5. You have just bought a car or home you can't afford.
6. Your secretary ignores you more than usual.
7. A member of the cleaning crew offers to help you get an interview with one of the other law firms in the building.

8. The Federal Express delivery person asks you what you are still doing here.
9. You've just had a performance review and the partners told you that you're doing a great job, everything's fine, and you're on the Partnership Track.

So long and "good luck in your future endeavors!"

Rodent Tale

A number of lawyers at a major Chicago firm were told that they would soon receive a letter from the managing partner that would ask each recipient "to relocate to a position of alternative professional responsibility outside the firm."

One associate found out about his termination well before the letter arrived. He said that another lawyer he knew came up to him on the street and told him he had heard of the associate's dismissal.

Rodent Tales

San Francisco's Thelen, Marrin, Johnson & Bridges announced that terminated associates would be notified via the office E-mail. Thirteen of the 110 associates who spent the entire morning watching their computer screens got the news that they had been let go.

When partners at Chicago's Winston & Strawn laid off a large group of associates, they did so by starting at the top floor and working their way down, floor by floor. As panic broke out around them, associates called their friends on lower floors with warnings and information such as "they are on floor forty-five now!"

▪ *Being the First to Say Good-bye* ▪

Primarily because associates live in constant fear of being terminated, many paranoid lawyers find new jobs even before they get axed by The Firm. Once the associate has lined up a new job, there is always the question of how to leave the old firm.

The associate could do the honorable thing and break the news personally to the partners. This doesn't usually go over very well, however, because partners want to be the first ones to say good-bye. Another consideration for an associate is that no severance pay is given to those who voluntarily quit The Firm.

Many associates decide to leave The Firm by forcing their own firing. This can be brought on by an attorney doing any one of the following:

1. Leaving the office one day to go home at five P.M.
2. Falling short of your billable hours goal two months in a row.
3. Simply saying "no" when a partner asks you to do a project without giving one of your usual lame excuses.
4. Walking through the office chanting "Attica! Attica! Attica!" **Caution:** Other associates are likely to join in and might end up being terminated when they don't intend to be.
5. Stop acting like an obsequious slob in the presence of partners.

Rodent Tale

A senior partner at a major New York firm had agreed to address the membership of the Manhattan Chamber of Commerce. Unfortunately, the partner forgot about the engagement until late on Friday evening when he saw the event on his calendar scheduled for the following Monday night. The partner, who had a weekend at the beach planned, called an associate to prepare the speech.

After listening to the partner describe what had to be done before Monday, the associate tried to explain that he and his girlfriend had already made plans to go away for the weekend. The partner interrupted the associate and emphasized that the assignment had to be on his desk Monday morning.

Come Monday morning, the partner found the freshly typed and neatly bound speech on his desk. On his way to a meeting at a client's office, the partner stuffed the speech in his briefcase without reading it. That night, standing before an audience of five hundred business executives, the partner delivered the speech.

Things were going smoothly, as the material was well written and the partner was making an excellent delivery of the text he was reading for the first time. Near the end of the speech, it reached a crescendo and the partner read:

> Before I leave you tonight, I want to share with you my ultimate vision for using the law not only to resolve disputes, but to create a new chapter in world history of mankind. A chapter of unparalleled peace and prosperity worldwide. To accomplish this, I will suggest that we . . .

The partner turned the page, curious himself to learn of this plan, only to find written on the paper before him: "IMPROVISE, YOU SON OF A BITCH."

▪ *Final Law Fibs* ▪

In conjunction with termination but before a lawyer leaves, The Firm always tries to get in one last Law Fib—just for old time's sake.

"You are being let go because of your substandard legal skills."

Translation: You are being let go because of a downturn in business.

"You are being let go because of a downturn in business."

Translation: You are being let go because of your substandard legal skills.

"You're doing a great job! Keep up the good work!"

Translation: You're fired!

"I went to the mat for you in the partnership meeting to try to save your job but there were too many people against me. I threatened to quit if they didn't keep you but they said they would sue me for breach of the partnership agreement."

Translation: I was beginning to feel threatened by you professionally so I told the other partners I would quit if they didn't fire you.

"It is time for you to relocate to a position of alternative professional responsibility outside The Firm."

Translation: Good luck in your future endeavors.

The Many Faces of the Of Counsel

The "Of Counsel" designation was traditionally reserved for distinguished (read: old) partners entering the twilight of their legal careers (read: losing it). The position allowed senior lawyers to curtail their workloads but at the same time maintain an association with The Firm. For these lawyers, the Of Counsel category is the law firm equivalent of being put out to pasture. For partners, it's a convenient way to avoid the unpleasantness (and inevitable lawsuit) resulting from unceremoniously dumping senior lawyers who have given their lives to The Firm.

Partners, knowing a good (and profitable) thing when they see it, have in recent years expanded the Of Counsel concept to include other attorneys who they don't know what to do with. Nowadays, one doesn't have to be old, senile, and a walking malpractice case to be an Of Counsel.

Old Lawyers Never Die,
They Just Become Of Counsel

"We'll still use his name and service the clients he brought in during his forty years of dedicated service to The Firm. We'd just rather not have him hanging around the office trying to do legal work. Have the old guy stop by the office once a month so we know he's still alive."

This Of Counsel's only real usefulness at The Firm is as a source of amusement to junior associates. They look up nineteenth-century court cases to see if he's listed as an attorney of record and stop by his office to confuse him by asking complex legal questions they know he can't answer.

When this Of Counsel finally does kick off, a one paragraph memo drafted by the receptionist is sent around the office as tribute to him for single-handedly building The Firm.

Not Quite Good Enough to Be a Partner

Sometimes known as a "permanent associate," this Of Counsel is a damn good lawyer and always does an excellent job but, let's face it, he's just not one of the boys. The Not Quite Good Enough to Be a Partner Of Counsel is the first person you call if you have a client with a difficult legal problem but the last person you call if there's an extra ticket to the ball game.

Although his legal skills clearly qualify him for partnership, he's not elected because, just before the vote, a senior partner asks: "Do we really want to share our profits with this dork and have him hanging around at our annual retreat?"

To discourage him from going to work at another firm, the partners change his status from associate to Of Counsel. They then convince him that being Of Counsel is really a big promotion. Even the Mail Guy knows it's The Firm's scarlet letter.

The Celebrity Attorney

This Of Counsel type is usually a former governor or U.S. senator. Despite never having practiced law and being forced to leave elective office under a cloud of public scandal, The Firm showcases him to clients and recruits, as well as in its promotional material.

This Of Counsel is paid a six-figure salary even though he's in the office less than the Old Of Counsel. His role is to bring business to The Firm in the form of dubious government contracts, go to lunch with partners' prospective clients, and make a few phone calls when a partner or client gets arrested for drunk driving or other embarrassing vice activities.

The Celebrity Attorney eventually leaves The Firm to run for president but fails to win a single primary.

Rodent Tales

The head of the corporate group at the Phoenix firm Streich Lang reportedly explained the need for certain changes at his firm by saying, "Life is like a caribou herd. When you get old or sick you drop behind and the wolves get you."

A lawyer from another firm said that some of his partners "don't retire even after they die," and that they continue to run The Firm from the grave. "Everyone keeps saying, 'What would Ira think, what would Ira think?' In a way, they're as influential when they're not there as when they were."

Death of a Lawyer

1. Lawyer found dead at desk.

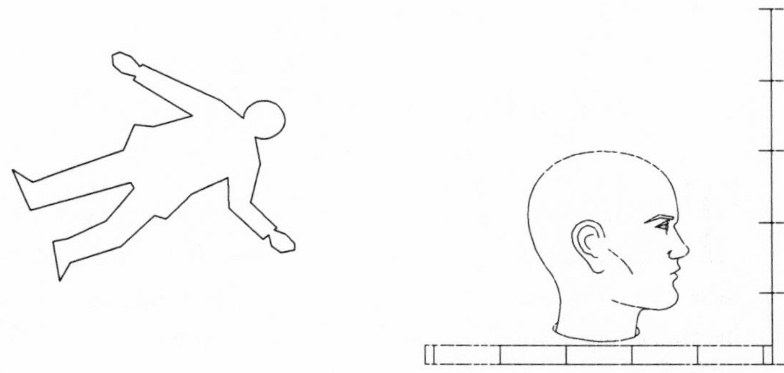

2. Autopsy shows cause of death to be overwork.

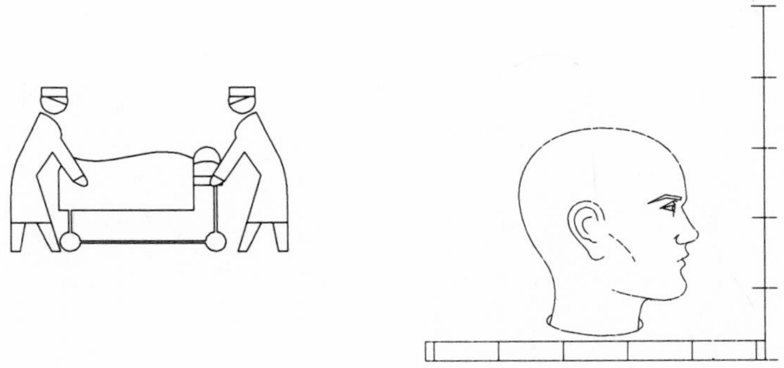

3. At the memorial service, partners, for the first time ever, say nice things about their departed colleague.

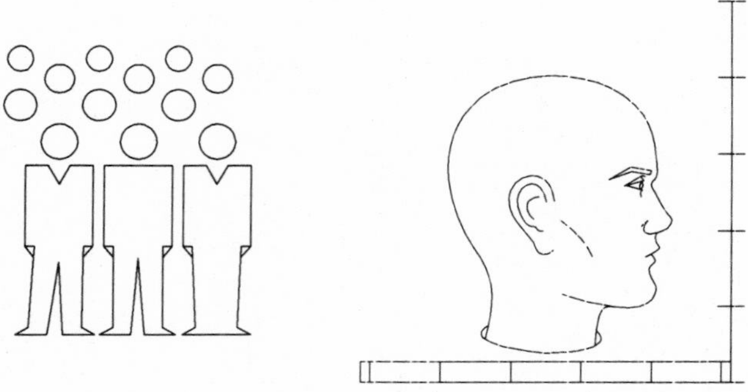

4. Surviving partners fight over now-vacant corner office and the right to service the deceased's clients.

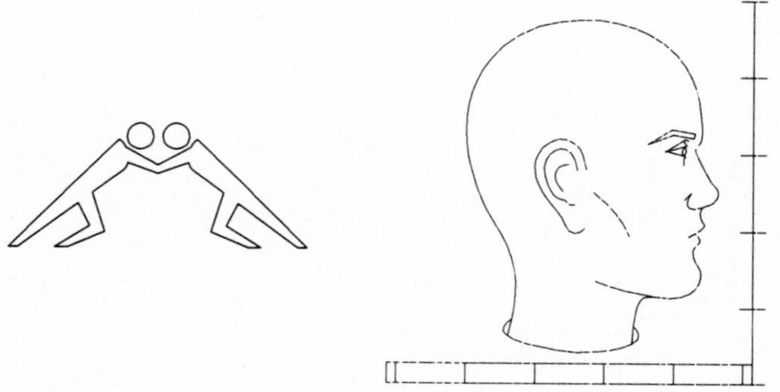

5. The Firm is hit with a big malpractice suit and the state bar is investigating. Partners decide to blame the whole thing on the dead lawyer.

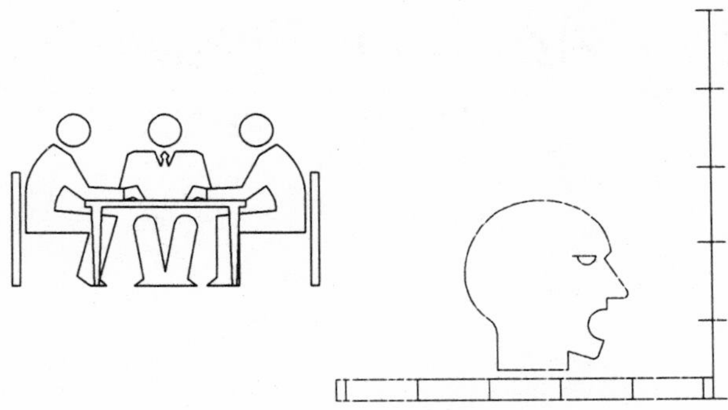

6. Deceased found guilty of malpractice. Surviving spouse left penniless. Lawyer is posthumously disbarred.

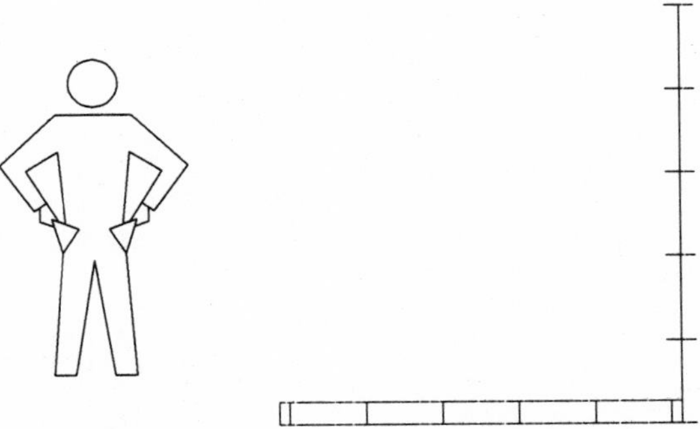

Advertisements: Attorney Products and Services

Continuing Legal Education Presents
POWER SCHMOOZING FOR LAWYERS

Tired of having to practice law to make it as a lawyer? Ever wonder why lazy and dim-witted colleagues succeed while you seem to get nowhere for all your hard work? Schmoozing is the answer and **Power Schmoozing for Lawyers** can change your life!

While it used to be vital for lawyers to learn traditional legal skills, today your success at The Firm depends more upon the ability to develop your own clients. By enrolling in **Power Schmoozing for Lawyers,** you'll learn:

- How to convince prospective clients they need to file law suits when no valid cause of action exists.
- Cocktail party small talk and false compliments clients love to hear.
- How to secure The Firm's tickets to the big game or hit show.
- Winning one liners such as: "Relax, I'm sleeping with the judge," and "Don't worry, my husband is governor."
- How to fake your way through an entire bankruptcy proceeding when you're an insurance defense hack.
- Valuable Vocabulary, including the correct usage of terms such as "chucker," "bogey," and "bow and stern," plus the names of small New England and Montana towns where you can claim to own a second home.

STOP LAWYERING AND START SCHMOOZING!
ENROLL NOW!! Call 555-8000

RENT-A-CLIENT

Are you scrambling to keep your job or making a push to become a partner? Would an impressive book of business complement your credentials? Call Rent-a-Client! *We can help.* We're the largest client-look-alike service in North America.

Our collection of professional actors and actresses are trained to impersonate the Chairman of the Board, CEO, or General Counsel of your choice.*

"Rent-a-Clients say the things partners love to hear."

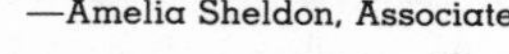

—Amelia Sheldon, Associate

"Hank's our boy!"

—Rent-a-Client's "General Counsel, Ford Motor Co."

"We want to buy the Dallas Cowboys."

—Rent-a-Client's "CEO, Nintendo Corporation"

"Is a one-million-dollar retainer enough to start?"

—Rent-a-Client's "Chairman of the Board, Exxon Corporation"

Special Offer: Order two Fortune 500 CEOs and get one in-house counsel absolutely free!

Call Today, Before You're Terminated! 1-320-CLIENTS

*For personal injury attorneys, we also rent victims. Just specify your area of the law and we'll provide a phony victim from the catastrophe du jour. Hurricane Andrew, Midwest flood, California earthquake and fire victims still available!

Exciting New Board Game

Throw Santa in the Slammer!

It's Christmas Eve, and you and your team of U.S. Justice Department officials raid Santa's workshop and try to **Throw Santa in The Slammer!**

See how many laws you can catch Santa violating while your opponents try to save Christmas by keeping Santa out of the pen. Argue whether Santa's helpers are undocumented workers and how much cargo his reindeer can carry without violating animal cruelty laws. Nab St. Nick as he enters the country without proper documentation and then breaks and enters into millions of homes. Does Santa's taking of cookies and carrots for his reindeer constitute petty theft? Will Santa spend Christmas Eve making children around the world joyful or sleep in a cold cell with his back to the wall? You decide!!!

Santa calls his attorney from the Big House

FUN FOR THE WHOLE FIRM!

$29.95

Wouldn't you like to bill all the hours wasted preparing documents in the time it takes to make a phone call?

You name the situation, we have the form.

FORMS R US

All the convenience and resources of a major law firm at a fraction of the cost. Simply plug in the names and our forms are ready for filing or signature. Charge clients by the word! Confuse opposing counsel with causes of action no one in your jurisdiction has ever heard of ($1.50 per provision). Include pages of useless language to bog down negotiations and run up legal bills. Order the same format used for the Rockefeller Center acquisition and adapt it for a $100,000 home loan. You bill the client for someone else's work! Special! Forms by the pound.* Bury your opponent!

1-320-FORMS R US

*All forms printed on recycled paper.

Are you a busy lawyer who needs to be in two places at the same time? Now you can be with Surrogate Lawyers

Our specially trained pseudoattorneys are there when you're not!

Kept from a business development dinner with a potential client because a meeting at the office is running late? Call us and we'll send out a Surrogate Lawyer who knows how to charm, con, and sign up new clients.

Need to put in a few extra hours at the office and it's time to go to your spouse's office party? Just request one of our attractive Surrogate Lawyers to do the things your spouse wants you to do. (Sober Surrogates available at slightly higher rates.)

Need a date for a dinner interview or Firm party? Our legal escort division has hundreds of Surrogates available for any social occasion (many different nationalities to choose from!)

Remember, *you* can bill clients for a Surrogate Lawyer's time.*

Call 1-320-826-3000 Today. Be there tomorrow.

"Here's my card. I'm an expert in every area of the law."

"Don't worry. The judge owes me a favor. We'll win big!"

"Yes, I am a lawyer at The Firm, but what's really important to me is my family."

*All Surrogate Lawyers are fully licensed to practice law by the State of Pennsylvania.

BERLITZ PARTNERESE

Speak Like a Partner in Six Weeks!

Why wait seven to ten years to learn Partnerese when we can teach you the key words and phrases partners use every day?

"Draft a purchase and sale agreement with all supporting documentation for the Paramount takeover but don't spend more than three hours on it."

"You'll never get that complaint filed in time if you take the afternoon off for that bone marrow transplant you supposedly need."

"You're doing a great job."

"Good luck in your future endeavors."

Also learn these exciting languages: International Tax Attorney, Mergers & Acquisitions Specialist Attorney, Power Partnerese, Falsely Accused of Malpractice Attorney, Interviewing/Forced Out Law Fibese.

Call Us: 1-320-TALK BIG

ARE YOU A LONESOME LAWYER TONIGHT?
CALL 555-FIRM*

Tired of 16-Hour Days, Unappreciative Clients, and Insolent Support Staff?

Are You an Associate With Clients, Partners, and the State Bar on Your Back?

Our* HOT *Partners with* HUGE *Firms are Waiting to Tell You What You Want to Hear!

"Great job!
Thanks for your help.
You'll make partner!"

"One thousand billable
hours a year is more
than enough.
Expect a big bonus."

"Relax. The Firm has
other clients and a
great malpractice
insurance policy."

*$350 PER HOUR FOR SENIOR PARTNERS. $250 PER HOUR FOR JUNIOR PARTNERS

Get Your Rodent Monthly

NO LAW FIB!

Keep up with all the latest news and developments at The Firm with . . .

The Rodent Newsletter

"The Official Underground Publication for Associates"

- -

Yes! I'm trapped in the rat race and want to run with *The Rodent!* Please enter my subscription.

Enclosed is my check for an annual subscription to *The Rodent* in amount checked below.

_____ **Power Partners:** $300 plus postage and handling

_____ **Puny Partners (admit it!), Libraries:** $25

_____ **Puny Partners at Puny Firms, Supreme Court Justices:** $20

_____ **Associates, Paralegals, Of Counsel, Sole Practitioners, Judges, In-house Counsel, Professors, Government Lawyers, Normal/Nonlaw People, and those not listed elsewhere:** $18

_____ **Law Students, Secretaries (except Senior Executive Secretaries), Prison Inmates, Disbarred (not including Power Partners), Kids Under Twelve:** $16

Outside the U.S., please add $4.00 to subscription rate.

Name: ____

Address: ____

City, State & Zip: _________________________________

SEND TO: RODENT PUBLICATIONS
2531 SAWTELLE BOULEVARD, #30, LOS ANGELES, CALIFORNIA 90064

Rodent Tale Sources

3. Lincoln Caplan, *Skadden: Power, Money, and the Rise of a Legal Empire* (New York: Farrar Straus Giroux, 1993), p. 147.
7. Ellen Joan Pollock, *Turks and Brahmins: Upheaval at Milbank, Tweed* (New York: Simon & Schuster, 1990), p. 20.
8. *Wall Street Journal,* June 1, 1994, p. B1.
9. *American Lawyer,* December 1989, p. 28.
11. *American Lawyer,* November, 1990, p. 54
12. Caplan, p. 158.
13. *American Lawyer,* November 1990, p. 54.
14. *Los Angeles Times,* August 13, 1992, p. B1.
19. *National Law Journal,* April 25, 1994, p. 1. *American Lawyer,* May 1994, p. 26.
20. Martin Mayer, *The Lawyers* (New York: Harper & Row, Publishers, 1966), pp. 76, 77.
26. Richard W. Moll, *The Lure of the Law* (New York: Viking, 1990), pp. 23, 24.
27. *New York Times,* June 14, 1991, p. C12.
29. Kim Isaac Eisler, *Shark Tank: Greed, Politics, and the Collapse of Finley Kumble, One of America's Largest Law Firms* (New York: St. Martin's Press, 1990), p. 109.
30, 31. *American Lawyer,* March 1989, p. 162.
36. *Washington Post,* August 31, 1993, p. B1.
40. Wendy Leigh, *Prince Charming: The John F. Kennedy, Jr. Story* (New York: Dutton, 1993), pp. 147, 148.
43. *American Lawyer,* March 1991, p. 22.
54. Eisler, p. 153.
57. *Wall Street Journal,* June 15, 1992, p. B5 (citing a *New York Law Journal* study).
71. *Washington Post,* June 5, 1992, p. D6.
72. *Los Angeles Times,* June 2, 1991, p. B1.
73. *American Bar Association Journal,* August 1993, p. 40.
76. *California Lawyer,* December 1990, p. 24.
81. *California Lawyer,* December 1990, p. 24.
94. *Los Angeles Magazine,* February, 1994.
97. *San Francisco Daily Journal,* May 4, 1994, p. 1.

98. Steven J. Kumble and Kevin J. Lahart, *Conduct Unbecoming: The Rise and Ruin of Finley, Kumble* (New York: Carroll & Graf Publishers, 1990), pp. 68, 69.
100, 101. *American Lawyer,* September 1991, pp. 2, 92.
103. *Asheville Citizen-Times,* October 10, 1994, p. 9A.
103. *Raleigh News & Observer,* June 6, 1994, pp. 1A, 20A.
106. *National Law Journal,* July 24, 1994, p. A6.
107. *Los Angeles Times,* June 2, 1991, p. B1.
111. *Washington Post,* June 8, 1992, p. D5. *National Law Journal,* July 11, 1994, p. 5.
112. *Washington Post,* June 8, 1992, p. 115 B5. *Los Angeles Times,* June 2, 1991, p. A1.
122. Mark Stevens, *Power of Attorney: The Rise of the Giant Law Firms* (New York: McGraw-Hill Book Company, 1987), pp. 70, 71.
123. *American Lawyer,* June 1993, p. 70.
132. Fisier, p. 110
135. *California Lawyer,* February 1993, p. 47.
136. *Washington Post,* December 13, 1993, p. D6. *Minnesota Journal of Law and Politics* (citing *San Jose Mercury News*), December, 1994, p. 9.
137. *American Bar Association Journal,* July 1993, p. 42.
140, 141. *Wall Street Journal,* May 13, 1994, p. B3; May 27, 1994, p. B1.
143. Caplan, pp. 33, 34.
156. Moll, p. 106.
162. *American Bar Association Journal,* September 1993, p. 47.
171. *American Lawyer,* June 1991, p. 61.
173. *American Lawyer,* March 1992, p. 26.
174. *California Lawyer,* March 1991, p. 24. Sheila Malkani and Michael Walsh, eds., *The Insider's Guide to Law Firms 1993–94* (Boulder, Col.: Mobius Press, 1993), p. 209.
176, 177. Stevens, pp. 179, 180.
184. *American Lawyer,* April 1991, p. 54. Stevens, p. 127.